PORSCHE
CARS WITH SOUL

PORSCHE
CARS WITH SOUL

GUI BERNARDES

THE CROWOOD PRESS

First published in 2017 by
The Crowood Press Ltd
Ramsbury, Marlborough
Wiltshire SN8 2HR

www.crowood.com

British Library Cataloguing-in-Publication Data
A catalogue record for this book is available from the British Library.

ISBN 978 1 78500 320 2

Photographic acknowledgements
All photographs are from the Porsche Archives, apart from the following:
Gui Bernardes: pages 7, 8, 9 10, 11, 154, 155, 156, 157, 158, 159, 160, 162, 164 (bottom), 166 (top), 167 (bottom), 169, 178, 181, 182, 183, 184, 185, 200 and 201
Jorge Bernardes: pages 2, 161, 163, 164 (top), 165, 166 (bottom), 167 (top), 168, 170, 171 and 172
Franco Lini (The GP Library): page 95
Jeff Zwart: page 147
Rupert Berrington: pages 149 and 150
David Colman: back cover and page 139

Typeset by Jean Cussons Typesetting, Diss, Norfolk
Printed and bound in India by Parksons Graphics

CONTENTS

DEDICATION

To my grandson Tomás, who is a dear autistic 10-year-old boy, hoping that one day he can read and understand this book about the cars he already recognizes and admires.

ACKNOWLEDGEMENTS

When I decided to write a book about Porsche, I was conscious that I would have to walk a long way and overcome the normal difficulties for anyone who is doing it for the first time.

I knew that I would need some help in different areas, but I was certain that the passion I have for the brand and the will to make this dream come true would certainly open some doors.

So I want to thank all those who in one way or another opened those doors for me: friends and Porsche enthusiasts who encouraged me to go on with my plans, when I had so many doubts in my mind; and mainly the Porsche Historical Archive in the persons of Jens Torner and Dieter Landenberger, who kindly gave me access to relevant information and provided most of the photos for the book.

Gui Bernardes

CHAPTER ONE

LOOKING FOR PORSCHE 'DNA' ORIGINS

19 JANUARY 2014, BRUSSELS, BELGIUM

It is not particularly cold on that Sunday morning when I approach Autoworld's building in Brussels, but the excitement of being about to see and touch some of the wonders created by Ferdinand Porsche and his successors almost makes me tremble with emotion as I cross the doorway crowned by the four Ferdinands. Having bought the ticket, I climb the metallic staircase that accesses the first floor where the expo is happening and what I see at a first glance confirms that the 1,250-mile (2,000km) trip that brought me here was well worth it. In a simple, but very well-achieved scenario, under soft and warm lighting, one can see a few dozen vehicles, which, for a lover of the Porsche brand, represent all of its history of genius, innovation, perseverance, style and success in automobile industry and motor sport.

Autoworld main entrance with posters announcing the exhibition.

The expo is divided into four zones, each one dedicated to its own Ferdinand. In the space pertaining to the founder, one can see magnificent examples of his technical expertise, in the diverse marques in which he worked before founding Porsche, such as a Lohner Mixte Hybrid model from 1901. This was the first hybrid car, with electrical engines on the front wheels powered by an electrical generator, which was in turn moved by a combustion engine.

There is a shining Austro-Daimler *Prinz Heinrich* model from 1910, in its

Lohner-Porsche Mixte Hybrid (1901).

immaculate white, which dominated the race for which it had been specially conceived, conquering the first three positions, with the victorious one being driven by Ferdinand Porsche himself.

From Electric to Electric. More than an hundred years separate the Porsche 918 from its hybrid ancestor.

Austro-Daimler
Prinz Heinrich
(1910).

Auto Union V16
Stromlinien-
wagen **(1937).**

Also on show is a fantastic Auto Union V16 *Stromlinienwagen* from 1937, a record-holding vehicle, which, with its aerodynamic lines and propelled by its enormous engine, sped up to 250mph (400km/h).

Several other interesting cars, like the famous KDF (Volkswagen), representing the innovative ideas and technical boldness of their creator, could be admired in this space, but it is not to them that I walk first. I want to see and contemplate immediately the one that was the first to embody what we call today the 'Porsche DNA'. I look around and there

ABOVE AND RIGHT:
Auto Union V16
Stromlinien-
wagen **(1937).**

it is, with its unmistakable silhouette and rounded shapes, not too thin but elegant, with a plunging hood between two outstanding headlights (like eyes peering at the roads from Berlin to Rome, the race for which it had been designed and built). It has a narrow and rounded cockpit, the better to slice through the air, and an accompanying unique profile of rear windows and descending aft section, all made up of smooth curves, with a lightness and at the same time a breathtaking dynamic.

I approach, enjoying the moment, while confirming the smoothness and beauty of its lines. I calmly pace around the mechanical sculpture so as to admire it fully. Its imperfect paint job, the rust that has taken over the rims of the headlights and the worn-out interior do not detract

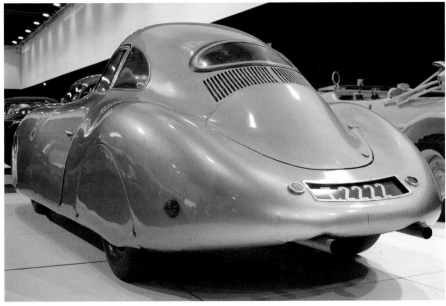

**Porsche 60K10
at Autoworld.**

from its value. In fact, they are witness to the many miles driven over more than seventy years.

If the 60K10[1] could speak, what fabulous tales it would have to tell! The impulse to touch and run my hand along that elegant shape is irresistible, and my hand rests softly over the metal … in that emotion-filled moment a vibrating wave runs up my arm, like an electric shock, and though it's not uncomfortable, I feel dizzy … all the cars at the expo rotate around me in an inebriating ballet and all of a sudden I feel as if I'm in another time, another space, another dimension …

CHAPTER TWO

THE BEGINNING

19 AUGUST 1939, STUTTGART-ZUFFENHAUSEN, GERMANY

While passing from the twilight in the Reutter Karosserie building to the exterior patio, pushed by two mechanics, I feel for the first time the slight irregularities of the ground through the thin tyres, half hidden by the fairings that contour my wheel arches. Four men[2] have just stepped out the nearby door. They are

Porsche 60K10 in Werk I yard in September 1939.

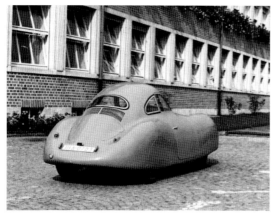

around me now, concentrating on the shapes of my bodywork and on its similar-
ity to the plans that left the drawing boards.

The four men have already exchanged opinions amongst themselves. The one
that appears to be the boss, with his piercing look, fierce moustache and hands
in pockets, has already walked twice around me. He seems pleased with what
he sees. In fact, this is not the first time we've been close to each other, because
he has already visited Reutter's[3] facilities several times during the bodywork
manufacturing process (slow and laborious, in which the masterful metalwork-
ers hammer the aluminium sheets to mould them to the contours of the wooden
moulds) to check on progress.

Aluminium alloys are materials that are more 'docile' and lighter than steel
alloys. They are a lot easier to work with, but hard to weld. These alloys, known
as duralumin, have been used in the aeronautical industry for some time. For
the aluminium atoms, which form the majority in this alloy, the moulding work
was not pleasant. Skilled artisans used vigorous but precise hammer blows to
change the structure of the alloy, so that it was possible to transform a flat and
expressionless metal sheet into a near sculptural shape. But I can't complain; the
final result was well worth the 'suffering' inflicted by the manufacturing process.

Lost in these thoughts, I shake when the doors are opened and two of the
four men get in. The one that sits at the wheel places his hand on the knob
that allows the reduction of air intake to the carburettors, then on the ignition
button. The pressure on the accelerator leads to the suction of gasoline, which
passes through the carburettors and enters the cylinders. The sparks fly from the
plugs, a first shudder passes through the entire structure, then a second, and
right after that the force of the exploding fuel expands the air in the combustion
chamber. The pistons are pushed, the crankshaft rotates on its bearings and the
engine shakes and vibrates, producing a characteristic and unmistakable sound.
The two men look at each other, confirming their mutual satisfaction and their
desire to confirm the dynamic capabilities of the machine. The clutch is pressed,
the gear lever engages first gear and after that the wheels start spinning. We're
moving, we're out of the factory's gate. The emotion rises as fast as the engine
revs. The air embraces smoothly the contours of the bodywork. I feel it pass light
and fast, and the speed increases even more.

The two men who stayed at the gate shake hands, satisfied and impressed,
as they watch the car speed along the Spitalwaldstrasse. Both of them have the
feeling that a beautiful success story in the automobile industry is about to begin!

The 60K10 project had been born with the objective of producing a
vehicle based on the mechanical elements of the KDF (Volkswagen),
but with more sporting characteristics so that it could participate in a
race due to be held for the first time in September 1939. This race would
be from Berlin to Rome, taking advantage for part of its route of the

recently built highway from Berlin to Munich. The project used part of the KDF's frame, but all of the bodywork was made in aluminium, drastically decreasing the weight to just 1,275lb (577kg). This light weight and the streamlined body shape, combined with an improved engine (larger valves, a higher compression ratio and twin Solex carburettors that increased power from 24 to 32bhp), allowed a top speed of 90mph (144km/h), which was remarkable at the time. Unfortunately, the Berlin–Rome race was never held, because of the beginning of hostilities in early September 1939 that led to World War II. However, Professor Ferdinand Porsche decided to go ahead with the construction of the two other previously planned units, and thus the three cars served as test vehicles in the following years.

The 60K10 remained in the service of the Professor himself, being driven most of the time by his chauffeur, Josef Goldinger. Even though it did not actually participate in competitions, it did continue to do justice to its design principles. In the many trips that the Professor took at the time, the car was seen travelling quickly along the German roads and highways, with records existing of one of those trips between Berlin and Fallersberg, the location where the KDF factory was being built. On this trip, the car performed at the extraordinary average speed, for the time, of 81mph (130km/h).

The second Porsche 60K10 built (c.1938/39).

The third 60K10 with an Austrian licence plate after being revamped (new grille, windscreen wipers under the windscreens, painted in silver).

The idea of building a light and aerodynamic car that could achieve remarkable performances, even though it used a small engine, had been set. Although the 60K10 was not formally a Porsche, but rather a sport variant of the KDF, it was in fact the first unit, in concept and shape, of the future marque from Zuffenhausen. The war that swept across Europe for almost six years postponed many of Ferdinand Porsche's projects and plans for the creation of his own brand, forcing him to transfer his company to Austria in 1945, due to the bombing to which the city of Stuttgart was being subjected. He found the ideal place to resite his company in the Austrian region of Carinthia, on the outskirts of the peaceful city of Gmünd, taking advantage of and increasing the existing buildings of a lumber mill in Karnerau. Here, he established design offices, regular offices, the production site, a canteen and even lodgings for some of the workers.

The Professor's office was right at the entrance, in a small pavilion adjacent to the guardhouse, next to the entry gate for the facility. This is where most of the engineers and designers were transferred, plus some production staff, that already worked at Zuffenhausen. Besides continuing to develop works for KDF and to guarantee the livelihood of the company, they also created projects in several other areas: farming machines; water turbines; generators; and even a project for a farm tractor.

However, after the war was over Professor Porsche was imprisoned in France. His son Ferry became the head of the company at Gmünd and did not let the plans of developing and selling automobiles carrying the family name die. Based on the projects preceding the war and always with the idea of using the mechanical components of the KDF (now named Volkswagen), the 356/1 project arose, with engineer Erwin Komenda still responsible for its development. Thus it was not strange that the new design had some similarities with the 60K10, although it was a totally different car, since it was a two-seater roadster, with a rudimentary canvas top. Mechanically, it employed several elements from the VW, including the suspension and the engine, though the engine was now rotated 180 degrees and in a central position, right behind the seats, with the gearbox at the back. This was the rebirth of the Professor's ideas applied in the famous and successful Auto Union made for competition before the war and resumed but never concluded in project 114.[4]

JUNE 1948, GMÜND, AUSTRIA

I can feel the fresh air from the fields that surround us, bringing with it the scent of trees and the mountains beyond. The wooden buildings that are nearby are bustling with activity. I can distinctly hear the familiar sound of hammers that are moulding the aluminium pieces, alternating with the sound of a revving engine being tested on a workbench. The idea that a drive awaits me, or better still, a test trip through the winding roads of Grossglockner, fills me with enthusiasm and I eagerly await its beginning.

Living as I did for a few years in the 60K10 has made me an addict of these road-devouring machines, which are almost inebriating for their drivers and passengers. It may seem odd that a simple aluminium atom is able to migrate from one car to another, allowing it to accompany the evolution of the 'species'

Porsche 356/1 with Ferry Porsche (left) and Ferdinand Porsche in Gmünd (1948).

and become a privileged witness of the experiences of trips, races, drivers, engineers, mechanics and extraordinary enthusiasts. As an atom of the most abundant metal on this planet, if left to chance, once my time in the bodywork or engine of a car is over, nothing would prevent me ending up as a simple kitchen utensil or soda can. However, thanks to a special gift whose origin I still haven't found, I do everything possible to get a 'host' whose interests ensure that he or she can transport me from one vehicle to another. Yes, because aluminium, like other metals, is present in the human body, which allows me, with some ability and resourcefulness, to pass from a car to a human and vice versa.

And this is how I find myself currently in the 356/1! How good it is to be here, on the first car that carries from its first moment the Porsche name. The seven letters shine proudly on the front of the hood between the fenders that house the headlights, already familiar in their position and shape. Three horizontal strips

TOP LEFT: **Porsche 356/1 interior with its single wide seat.**

TOP RIGHT: **The 356/1's simple dashboard.**

BELOW: **The 356/1 top view clearly shows the narrow ventilation slots on the rear hood.**

The 356/1 VW engine in its central position just behind the wide seat.

between the indicators beautify the front, without any openings, simple and functional. The windshield without a metallic frame gives an even lighter air to the car, whose simple but comfortable interior invites the driver and passenger to sit on a single wide seat.

The concern to keep the weight as low as possible is reflected in the austerity of the equipment. A simple speedometer fills the dashboard on the driver's side, surrounded by the buttons that command the lights and windshield wipers. On the passenger's side there is a glovebox, whose lid incorporates a clock. Immediately behind the wide seat, a long rear lid with fluid lines covers the engine until the rear bumper, with a remarkably original and simple solution found to allow the engine to 'breathe' – two lines of narrow and elegant slots along the sides of the rear hood, almost invisible but efficient. The rear fenders accentuate the lines of the hood, ending in beautiful tail lights near the bumper. All the elements on this aluminium bodywork connect to a tubular frame, allowing the total weight to be 1,330lb (602kg). Combined with 40bhp delivered by the optimized VW engine, this will certainly result in an impressive performance.

That is certainly what Ferry Porsche intends to show to his visitor[5] on this demonstration trip of the car he had long desired to see created. Nothing could show the car's performace better than the drive to Zell am See, a small city of dazzling beauty near Lake Zeller, where the Porsche family had chosen to take up residence after leaving Stuttgart. To get there from Gmünd one must cross the highest mountain in Austria – the Grossglockner – which rises up to 12,660ft (3,798m). The mountain road unravels along 30 miles (48km), reaching its highest point at 8,346ft (2,504m), winding through the hillsides, with thirty-six hair-

Porsche 356/1 in Austrian landscape (1948).

pin bends and slopes over 10 per cent. It is such a fantastic ground on which to test the behaviour of a car, as much in agility as in power and braking.

But before arriving at Grossglockner we must travel 43 miles (70km) on a less demanding road, passing by Trebesing, Stall and Lainach, where some straights allow the car to reach close to 87mph (140km/h). This makes Ferry Porsche smile and look at his companion, who answers his look with one word: 'Perfekt'. Having arrived at Winklern, one then takes the fabulous road towards the Grossglockner. The scenery is strikingly beautiful, but Ferry is now committed to get from the 356/1 all that it can give, accelerating heavily on the straights and taking the turns aggressively. The car's performance and near perfect weight distribution inspire confidence and invite a sporting style of driving.

One hairpin bend quickly follows another. There is no snow on the road, but many of the highest mountain peaks are still cloaked in white mantles, making the scenery even more enjoyable. We approach the highest point at a good rhythm, but just after passing the Fuscher Lake I can feel the back end slipping out a bit, which is quickly corrected by Ferry Porsche's superb driving skills. After some more curves, we approach the famous guard house, before the road on the right to the Edelweißspitze overlook. However, Ferry intends to go to Zell am See and come back to Gmünd while it is still daylight, so we start the steep descent

The first 356/2 outside the factory in Gmünd (1948). The 3561/1 roadster can be seen in the background.

towards Lake Zell instead. The pleasure of travelling on such a beautiful road in a machine to match makes me feel overwhelmingly fortunate.

Having arrived at Zell am See, we pass the aviation field. Up ahead is the turn-off to Schüttgutweg, the access road to the Porsche family property, but we go straight on and stop at Elisabeth Park, by the beautiful and calm lake. After a short rest, the 356/1's engine can be heard again and now we're on the reverse route to Gmünd. How fantastic this 'life' will be in the 356/1!

A Porsche 356/2 with wool tufts on its body ready to leave Gmünd facilities for an aerodynamic test.

On this day, Ferry Porsche became even more convinced of how valid everyone's work on this project had been and how promising the end result was. The Porsche family had finally built its own car, which they could introduce to the world and launch their company into automotive history.

When Professor Ferdinand Porsche (now released from imprisonment) returned to Gmünd, he was impressed with the work developed under his son's guidance, namely this 356/1 and the Formula One car *Cisitalia*, developed from an order for Italian businessman Piero Dusio.[6] He gave both cars his approval and stated that he would not have made them differently himself. Meanwhile, Ferry Porsche had not limited himself to launching the 356/1 project, since almost at the same time the first 356/2 was created. Unlike the 356/1, which was intended to be a showcase for Porsche know-how, the 356/2 was envisaged as a (small) series production. The tubular-frame construction of the 356/1 would be too expensive for series production, plus only having two seats would limit

The 356 test car in front of the building housing Prof. Ferdinand Porsche's office at the entrance of the Gmünd factory.

its appeal to a wider automotive market, so the 356/2 was designed as a 2+2 with room for luggage. Ferry was also mindful that he should use the maximum number of VW components, with whom he had preferential agreements, as a way of minimizing production costs.

It was under these premises that the 356/2 was born, as both a coupé and a cabriolet, being inspired in its shape and structure by the 60K10 from before the war. The bodywork was still made of aluminium, through the same processes, allowing on the one hand a low weight to be maintained and on the other avoiding new investment in expensive moulds and machinery. The mechanical elements in the steering, suspension and engine were of VW origin, with the engines being modified to obtain a better performance. The good impression that the 356/1 and 356/2 made on several motoring journalists who tested them led to the first flow of orders, the initial one having been placed by Rupprecht von Senger.

From 1948 to 1950, forty-six cars were built at Gmünd, which exceeded Ferdinand and Ferry Porsche's initial expectations, given the difficulties in obtaining raw materials and components. This number included both coupés and cabriolets, since the open version gathered clients straight away. A unit of each version built at Gmünd was exhibited at the Automotive Show in Geneva in March 1949. There, visitors could appreciate the cars of the new brand, which were praised in specialist newspapers and magazines for their elegant and sporting lines, but also for their performance.

It was, in fact, very difficult to remain indifferent to the coupé's silhouette, with its rounded and fluid shape, which set it apart from other sporting brands of the time. And the cabriolet, with the small variations between the coach builders that assembled them,[7] was also a synonym of elegance and distinction, with a precise and rigorous build.

As a result of the success of these cars, it soon became clear that the almost handcrafted production at Gmünd could not meet the demands of the market, even though most of the final assembly of the cars was subcontracted. Ferdinand and Ferry started to prepare the return of the company to Stuttgart, where the working conditions would be much more favourable. Since the factory was still occupied by American troops, they had to resort to renting a building close by, as well as also renting space at Reutter Karosserie, with whom they made a contract to produce 500 bodies. The Glaser company also obtained a contract to produce the 356 cabriolets.

Production commenced at the end of 1949, although with some significant changes from the cars made at Gmünd. The bodies would now be made of steel, since there were not enough personnel with the necessary experience to mould and weld aluminium in Stuttgart in the amounts needed. It was also necessary to invest 200,000DM in the manufacture of the moulds required for stamping the components, with most of the money for this being obtained by payment up front for firm orders. The first 356 built in Stuttgart was finished on Maundy Thursday, 1950, and remained in the possession of the man who had most wanted and deserved it, Ferry Porsche.

3 SEPTEMBER 1950, SCHLOSS SOLITUDE, GERMANY

It is with great enthusiasm that, looking around me, I see several 356s aligned in front of an elegant palace. The owners of these cars have gathered on the grand staircase, which divides into two harmonious curves, in order to pay homage to an emerging automotive brand, but most of all to its mentor on his seventy-fifth birthday. Now in poor health, the Professor seems to have grown younger as a result of seeing and feeling the affection of these first clients and brand enthusi-asts. This pleasant day culminates in the delivery of a special gift for the illustrious birthday man: a beautiful black 356 Gmünd coupé. I feel a strong emotion when the Professor opens the door and takes the wheel. It is a special time, having the Professor so close and being able to share some trips with him.

Ferdinand Porsche at Schloss Solitude celebrating his seventy-fifth birthday.

FAR RIGHT:
Professor Ferdinand Porsche was impressed and touched with the homage he received on his seventy-fifth birthday.

This 356 would come to be known by its nickname, 'Ferdinand', and would be used as a test vehicle for the several improvements that were introduced in the series production cars during the following years. The event at the Palace of Solitude, besides its more personal side, was the starting point of what would become a way of being for the brand, gathering owners together in clubs, first in Germany, and then throughout Europe.

Ferdinand Porsche with his 356 'Ferdinand' at Katschberg in Austria (1950).

CHAPTER THREE

GOING INTO RACING: THE 1950s

24 JUNE 1951, CIRCUIT DE LA SARTHE, LE MANS, FRANCE

I feel that the 356 SL is giving all that its driver is asking of it. The speed attained along this long straight is impressive – the trees on the side of the road go by quickly and even though the more powerful cars overtake us with ease, in the 1100cc class there is no one that can keep up with us. To prove this point, we approach and overtake a small Simca 8 Sport and a DB/Panhard at 100mph (160km/h).[8] The heavy braking at the end of the Hunaudières Straight does make us oscillate a little, when we enter the Mulsanne corner, the place where the D338 and D140 national roads intersect, which is followed by a new straight cut by a slight turn until the Indianapolis curves. Before these curves, the speed rises again above 94mph (150km/h) and the adrenalin rises too during braking and the following approach to the right/left sequence. All this is dealt with smoothly by the driver, who is fully confident in the manoeuvrability and handling of the 356.

A few minutes before the start of the race, Auguste Veuillet (facing the camera) and Edmond Mouche in white overalls stand beside the 356 SL.

TOP LEFT: **The 356 SL after the start of the 24 Hours of Le Mans (1951).**

TOP RIGHT: **The 356 SL at the Dunlop curve.**

But after a short straight we are already dealing with another of the circuit's famous curves – the Arnage, which results in a 90-degree turn towards the city of Le Mans. (It is on the sand barriers placed there as protection, as well as on the Indianapolis curves, that many cars end the race ingloriously.) We are now approaching the curve of Maison Blanche, where we are surprised by an Aston Martin that is stopped on the track after having spun. However, a quick trajectory correction, without lifting the foot from the accelerator, allows us to pass untouched, with the chassis dealing well with the weight transfer this causes. Now we're continuing towards the finish straight. When we get there, Auguste Veuillet moves over to the right, because we are going into the pit lane to refuel.

It is fantastic to appreciate the enthusiasm of the spectators on the stands, the frenetic work of the mechanics taking care of their machines, the fatigued air of the drivers handing the cars over to their teammates, who are waiting anxiously for the moment to return to the track. Stopped in our pit, the mechanics rush to fill up the tank through the refuelling opening that crosses the front hood, while another cleans the windshield, quite dirty with oil and mosquitoes gathered during our last laps on the circuit. Auguste Veuillet is surrendering the wheel to Edmond Mouche, who is talking with Ferry Porsche sitting on the wall of pit lane, and that made it a point to live inside the first 24 Hours of Le Mans in the make's history.

After this short stop I'm off for another shift full of emotion, now driven by Mouche. We go under the Dunlop Bridge, then into the Tertre Rouge corner, which gives access to the long Hunaudières Straight that is passed once again at great speed. I will not be bored in any of the 210 laps completed throughout the race, with the last one being naturally the most thrilling, because we achieved our objectives, winning our class and running 1,775 miles (2,840km) without major issues, at an average speed of 73.5mph (118.36km/h).

The joy of all who took part in this adventure was enormous and the reward for the boldness, perseverance and the quality of the work done was thoroughly deserved. There was only one sorrow, that the Professor was no longer among us too share that joy,[9] but his knowledge, charisma and will to win lived on through the team.

Auguste Veuillet had not forgotten that, when he had challenged Professor Porsche at the 1950 Paris Auto Show (where the marque's two models were on display) to participate in the already legendary race, that the latter had questioned him about what would be the maximum and average speeds required to be able to fight for victory in the 1100cc class. Taking the numbers given by Veuillet, the Professor did some quick mathematics with his calculus ruler and answered: 'Yes, it can be done. It will be difficult but it is possible.' Veuillet had recently been designated the importer of Porsche vehicles to France, which was the reason for his presence with members of the Porsche family at the Paris Auto Show, where the Porsche cars once again attracted the praise and attention of both the public and the specialist press alike.

Professor Porsche was finally convinced to take part in the 24 Hours of Le Mans after being visited in October 1950 by his friend Charles Faroux,[10] the race director, who advised him that even a class victory would be extremely valuable publicity for the new marque, whose fame was beginning to spread beyond Germany. Ferry Porsche was also there and was truly pleased by his father's decision, although he was conscious of the extra labour that it meant for everyone, since there were only eight months in which to get the cars prepared to race on the asphalt of the La Sarthe's circuit.

Auguste Veuillet and Edmond Mouche achieved victory in the class up to 1100cc with the 356 SL at the first deployment of a Porsche in Le Mans (1951).

356 coupé and cabriolet at Paris Auto Show (1950).

Even though that at that time all the production was already based in Stuttgart, the choice of the cars for the race fell on two that had been built at Gmünd, since their aluminium bodywork represented a considerable advantage in terms of weight, with a saving of 350lb (157kg). The cars were improved, not only from an aerodynamic point of view, with the fairings over the wheels being particularly evident, but also on the mechanical level, with the improved cooling of the brakes and an increase of the engine's power to 46bhp. The model with these changes was designated as 356 SL (*Sports Leicht*) and it was even introduced with a four-page catalogue, since by the ACO's[11] regulations it was mandatory that the enrolled cars were available to the public, which the leaflet confirmed, also mentioning the availability to accept orders.

The plans to enter the Le Mans race with two cars meanwhile went awry, since in the practice session, one of them (no.47) suffered an accident and it was impossible to repair it in time for the race. Despite a poor start, no.46 achieved the success all were wishing for. The race left such an impression on Ferry Porsche that it became a priority for the brand for many years and ever since then there has not been a single year that

The two 356 SLs being prepared for the race at George Després' garage in Teloché. This garage near the circuit served as Porsche 'headquarters' from 1951 until 1981.

has not seen Porsche cars, in the hands of official drivers or private ones, competing on the French track.

In October of that year there was another important event for the marque, when two 356 SLs, driven by Petermax Müller, Huschke von Hanstein, Walter Glöckler, Richard von Frankenberg and Hermann Ramelow, broke several world speed records in the 1100 and 1500cc classes on Montlhéry's speed track. A new record for the distance travelled in 72 hours stood out: 6,855 miles (11,030km), at an average speed of 95.21mph (153.2km/h). This record was set on the morning of the Paris Auto Show's opening, where the car was driven and put on show with enormous success. The 1500cc engine, which generated 72bhp, would come to form the basis of a more civilized version, when it was used in the series production cars with power set at 60bhp. This was the

Record-breaking in Montlhéry (1951).

The 356 SL on the steep banking of the Montlhéry track.

beginning of the philosophy that has stood the brand in good stead, to test new solutions on the track and consequently apply them to series production.

13–16 AUGUST 1952, LIÈGE, BELGIUM

One hundred and six cars parked on the courtyard of the beautiful Palais de Justice on Saint-Lambert Square in Liège are ready to start the toughest road race in Europe, the Liège–Rome–Liège rally, also known as the Marathon de la Route. It is considered by many to be more demanding and shattering than the Mille Miglia, as it takes place over five days and totals over 3,125 miles (5,000km) of difficult roads, including the most challenging Alpine passes. Competitors have to do the whole round trip between the two cities with almost no time to rest, because the average speed of 37.3mph (60km/h) required in most sections is impossible to fulfil if stops are made to sleep or take normal meals.

It is a prerogative of the organizers to ensure that there are no competitors finishing without penalties and as in 1951 the winning team (Johan Claes/Jacques Ickx in a Jaguar XK120) had managed this feat, the rally this year has been increased by 250 miles (400km) and the average speed requirement increased

Three Porsche 356 SLs ready for the 1952 Liège–Rome–Liège, also known as the Marathon de la Route.

from 31.1 to 37.3mph (50 to 60km/h) to ensure that the situation would not be repeated. The race is fact overwhelming for machines and men, totalling 3,212 miles (5,168km), with fifty-four time-control zones, expressed on the map as a rough figure of eight, with Liège at one end and Rome at the other. The cars will run successively through Belgium, Luxembourg, France, Italy, Germany and Belgium again.

To carry out this route drawn by the organizers, it is necessary to cross the Alps in both directions, overcoming a number of peaks that are well known to the majority of the teams: the Croix de Fer (6,846ft/2,054m); the Galibier (8,383ft/2,515m); the Izoard (7,740ft/2,322m); the Vars (6,923ft/2,077m); the Cayolle (7,630ft)/2,289m); and the Allos (7,380ft/2,214m), which also have to be crossed on the return journey. In addition to these, we have also to overcome: the Pordoi (7,353ft/2,206m); the Falzarego (6,943ft/2,083m); the Costalunga (5,750ft/1,725m); the Stelvio Pass (9,040ft/2,712m); and the more than feared Gavia (8,596ft/2,579m), which will need to be overcome at dusk or even over-night. To accomplish the entire journey without penalties, it would need to be done in 88hr 45min, which is practically impossible. Every second exceeding the time allowed for each of the twelve sections of the rally corresponds to one penalty point.

Among the 106 cars participating, the largest contingent is from Porsche with 16 teams, which is in fact a great number for a marque so new to motor racing. Competing brands are: Jaguar; Aston Martin; Bristol; Healey, MG; Citroën, Peugeot; Simca; and Fiat, among others. The more competitive Porsches are the usual 356 SLs with aluminium bodywork and a 70bhp engine, and I will have the pleasure of experiencing this enormous challenge in the car of Huschke von Hanstein, the well-known public relations manager of the brand, who shares the steering wheel with Petermax Müller.

It is going to be a tough task for the team, because von Hanstein, although a good driver, is not at the same level as the best and his experience of this type of event is limited. Another 356 built in Gmünd will be driven by a renowned driver with a relevant racing history, Helmut Polensky, the last winner of the similarly difficult Rallye des Alpes, which also uses some of the Alpine roads we will have to deal with over the coming days.

The actual start of the race will be in Spa at 23:00. We're heading there now, applauded along the way by thousands of spectators. The start procedure is spectacular, because the departure flag releases simultaneously a group of three cars every 3 minutes. Side by side these accelerate to the maximum, much to the delight of the crowd, as they head for Grenoble, 468 miles (750km) away. The first timed section, between Grenoble and Saint-Michel-de-Maurienne, is driven under scorching heat, making life even more difficult for machines and drivers, especially when crossing the Croix de Fer pass.

Along the route, we come across many broken or crashed cars, confirming *how hard the event is. Among the unfortunate ones are the winners of the previous race, whose Jaguar has hit a road milestone on the edge of a precipice, fortunately without adverse consequences for the drivers, who wave to us as we pass by them.*

The time controls are so close and the average speed so demanding for the type of roads travelled, even for the fastest teams, that only very short stops to eat or rest are possible. The average speed required between Guillaumes and Nice has been reduced to 31.1mph (50km/h), with the organization taking into account the fact that today is a public holiday with plenty of traffic. So we could gain a bit of time, to use for a longer stop at the control in Nice, located on the Promenade des Anglais, where in addition to refreshments and food, there is even champagne, served graciously to the competitors by the most beautiful girls of the Riviera (according to the comments exchanged between von Hanstein and Müller, who are rightly enjoying this brief respite in hostilities). We also learn that despite only having driven less than one-quarter of the race, more than one-third of the teams have given up!

We are now in Italy, after some time lost in the formalities at the border's customs, although this is not enough reason for the organization's clock to be a little more forgiving. The time controls are now livelier, with Italian fans applauding all competitors, but especially their compatriots. At these controls, refreshments and sandwiches that riders will eat in the following miles are always delivered. The fight against the stopwatch continues relentlessly and penalties keep accumulating for most teams.

We enter Pisa at dawn, then continue towards Florence, Siena and Viterbo, before arriving in Rome. It is a torrid heat when we get there, but von Hanstein rejoices when he is informed that we are among the nine teams that have been able to reach the middle of the rally without any penalty. The 'sister' car of Polensky–Schlüter is also in this group of heroes, where there are also three Lancia Aurelias (one of which is driven by the famous Maglioli), a Stanguellini Fiat, a Jaguar, a Ferrari and a Frazer Nash of the only English team competing.

But in reality we still have more than half of the route ahead of us, because even though Rome is the southernmost point on the road map, the halfway point is reached only at the control of Ferrara, already on the return trip to Liège. On the way to Ferrara, taking advantage of the highways, we can gain some time, which will allow us to get some rest at that control point. We do a great portion of this section in the company of Polensky and the Frazer Nash of Moore-Gott, making the most of the high speeds that the cars can achieve.

The following sections, passing by Costalunga and Bolzano, are proving to be more difficult than expected, with several teams suffering accidents, possibly due to fatigue after 52 hours of racing and the poor condition of some of the roads. The next section towards Stelvio sees the withdrawal of frontrunners Ferrari and Frazer Nash. After the Pordoi pass there is no competitor without penalties.

After the Alpine passes of Stelvio and the feared Gavia, the Lancia of Maglioli leads, 2min 57sec ahead of the Porsche of Polensky. In the first ten cars there are two more Porsches, driven by Strasse and Engel. Our performance has dropped a little and we are now off the 'honour board', although all forty-three teams still in the competition, after the passage through the Dolomites, are worthy of the highest admiration.

But the second passage through the French Alps causes a change of leader and drama for the Italians, because Maglioli's Lancia is forced to retire with mechanical problems, thus leaving Polensky in the lead. Von Hanstein is now trying to regain some time and we climb a few places in the classification, when we get the fastest time at the control point of Vars. The speed of the Porsches continues to impress, to the amazement of some in more powerful machines – the fastest 356s have always been among the first four classified in the mountain passes.

But the final difficulty for the weary competitors is yet to come: the Galibier pass is submerged in a dense fog and here Polensky definitely outrides the competition, incurring a penalty of only 12 seconds despite the extremely difficult conditions. His superb drive is highlighted by the fact that the second classified in this section is penalized 4min 9sec. After this section, there are three Porsches in the top four positions, with the Jaguar of LaRoche in the second position.

Porsche 356 SL of Polensky/ Schlüter, winner of the 1952 Liège– Rome–Liège.

But there are still 1,243 miles (2,000km) until the finish line, which is finally reached on Sunday afternoon. The arrival of Polensky and Schlüter is acclaimed by many enthusiasts, impressed with the performance of the winning car, but also with the global result of Porsche. The company has five cars in the top ten, with us closing this group after the final recovery by von Hanstein. Polensky's victory is a cause for celebration by the whole team, as the ultimate advantage of 7min 9sec over the Jaguar in second place reflects the outstanding performance of both the car and its drivers. All twenty-four teams that finished the race, weary after five days of this difficult adventure, head for a well-deserved rest. Before these brave drivers reach the hotels, I will also be recovering my strength, parked in this magnificent square below a starry sky and surrounded by a mild temperature, in a comforting calm after five days that were exhausting, but well worth living!

The awards ceremony of the Liège–Rome– Liège 1952 took place on Monday afternoon, 17 August. For the winning drivers, this was a very special moment, finding themselves rewarded for all the effort they had made. For Porsche, the victory had a very special flavour, not only because it demonstrated the value of the cars, which was clearly reflected in the results achieved, but also because it was the first official overall win of the marque since it began participating in motor racing. The Stuttgart-Zuffenhausen company was becoming increasingly known and admired, both in sporting circles and among the general public. This recognition was reflected in a growing volume of sales. In 1952, the factory produced over 1,000 cars, initiating the slogan later adopted by the brand: 'Win on Sunday, sell on Monday.'

2 MAY 1954, BRESCIA, ITALY

The most famous road race in the world takes place every year in early May in Italy. It is the legendary Mille Miglia, which always attracts the best drivers. Thousands of enthusiastic fans line the route, which departs from Brescia in the north, towards Rome, passing through Verona, Vicenza, Padua, Ferrara, Pescara, then returning to Brescia via Viterbo, Florence, Bologna, Modena and Parma. It is a 1,000-mile race (more exactly 998 miles/1,606km), that the competitors run non-stop to try to carry out the course in the shortest time possible.

The prestige of the event is such that there are more than 400 cars entered, from the smallest (such as the Isetta 'egg' and the Citroën 2CV) to the most powerful machines like the Ferrari, Lancia, Maserati and Aston Martin. As usual, the Italians are the great rulers of this race, which Ferrari has won for the last six years. This year the main contenders for victory are:

* *Lancia, appearing in force with four 3.3-litre cars for Ascari (current Formula One world champion), Taruffi, Castellotti and Valenzano*
* *Ferrari with four 5-litre cars for Farina, Maglioli and two of the Marzotto brothers, Paolo and Giannino (winner in 1950 and 1953)*
* *Aston Martin with two cars for Parnell and Collins.*

All these cars belong to the class Sport +2-litres and are accompanied by many others entered by private drivers either in this class, or in Grand Tourism and Tourism. Porsche, besides being represented in GT class with a 356 for Richard von Frankenberg/Heinrich Sauter, is putting its hopes for a good classification in a 550 Spyder, entered in the class Sport 1.5-litres for Hans Herrmann/Herbert Linge. And it is with these master drivers that I will live this blistering, unique and reckless race!

After the scrutineering, which takes place in the Piazza de la Vittoria watched by thousands of spectators, the departure time for the first car is given as Saturday at 21:00. Competitors leave one by one, every minute, with the competition number of each car corresponding to its departure time. The first ones to leave are the smaller displacement cars and thus the potential candidates to victory are the last to leave Brescia, almost with the first of Sunday's rays of sun emerging on the horizon.

Our 550 Spyder (chassis no.08) has been given no.351, which logically implies a departure and a night ride almost up to Pescara. The event has been well prepared by the team, with previous reconnaissance having been carried out. Herbert Linge, who is also an experienced driver and mechanic, will be an alert navigator in this race, indicating the directions and the most dangerous points to Hans Herrmann. He has a notebook he calls his 'road bible' and a visual communication system (as oral communication becomes impossible above the engine noise) consisting of three boards of different colours, green, yellow and red, to indicate the driving situation.

After the departure of the car that precedes us, a few seconds after 03:50 it is our turn to climb the ramp located in the Viale Venezia and wait for the flag drop (given since the first race in 1927 by the famous Signor Castagneto), which will set us free towards Verona. Despite the hour, hundreds, if not thousands, of spectators line the road and applaud the competitors. At 03:51, Herrmann accelerates down the ramp and we are off on another extraordinary adventure.

Hans Herrmann and Herbert Linge at the start of the 1954 Mille Miglia in the 550 Spyder.

Herbert Linge reads his roadbook before giving vital information to Hans Herrmann in the 1954 Mille Miglia.

The first part of the race to Verona is one of the fastest around the course, as there are many straight lines and the type 547 engine, designed by Ernst Fuhrmann and now used in the 550, delivers all its 110bhp, which allows an average of 94mph (150km/h). Drivers 'only' have to pay special attention to any degraded roads and the railway crossings that are found along the route. The railway crossings can be a serious problem for competitors because some may be closed, leading to an inevitable waste of time, but also because any major gap between the road and the rails can cause serious damage to the cars as they pass over at high speed. To minimize these situations, there is an 'understanding' between the race organizers and the Italian Railways, so that employees close the gates with less notice than is normal (sometimes only when they spot the arriving train!). A marshal is placed a few dozen metres before each crossing to show a flag to competitors, indicating if the gates are open or closed. Linge has also marked in his notes where the worst gaps between the road and the rails are, in order to notify Herrmann with the corresponding coloured cardboard.

The sun has just risen and now we arrive at the time control in Pescara, with 391 miles (629km) covered after 4 hours of racing. Following Pescara, we have a slower and mountainous route, which leads us to Rome. We are approaching the town of Chieti, running at over 100mph (160km/h), taking advantage of a small straight on the winding route. Linge is consulting his 'bible' and signals Herrmann that we are approaching a railroad crossing, which is of the 'easy' type, so he shows him the green board. The straight ends so Herrmann brakes slightly, as the curve that follows is a fast one but with no forward visibility, and after that comes the railroad crossing ... closed! Herrmann sees the train approaching and, realizing that he has no chance to stop before the gates, accelerates, raises his right arm and pushes Linge's helmet down as far as possible, while at the same time lowering his own head, and it is thus that the 550 passes underneath the gates to the amazement of both the spectators and the crossing marshal.

The 550 Spyder passes underneath the railroad crossing gates while the train arrives at great speed!

The marshal who should be indicating the closed crossing a few dozen metres behind is also stunned, leaning against the gates. He surely sends prayers to the Madonna, giving thanks that everything went well, while Hermann and Linge, recovered from the frightening moment, may well also give thanks (perhaps to St Christopher!) for their safe delivery, as they continue on the road to Rome.

At the time control in Rome, 6 hours into the event and a little more than halfway through the course, fatigue begins to make itself felt. The most difficult part of the race is yet to come, but thousands of spectators cheer us on and it is with renewed courage that we leave the control. It is virtually impossible to know our ranking, due to the staggered departure procedure, but we learn that we are now 15 minutes ahead of our main opponent to victory in the class, the OSCA of Cabianca, which departed Brescia 8 minutes before our 550 and which we passed on the road a few miles behind.

The route is now much more demanding, especially for the less powerful cars, as towards Viterbo we must overcome the Radicofani pass. After this difficulty, we move towards the beautiful city of Florence, whose magnificent streets are packed with racing enthusiasts. Then we are into the next challenge, crossing the Apennines over the Futa and Raticosa passes. Herrmann manages to keep a very lively pace along the mountain roads and soon we are in Bologna. In the final part of the leg, the organizers have revised the route this year to pass through Mantua, where Italian racing driver Tazio Nuvolari died in 1953. Tribute is thus paid to him and there is even a special prize for the fastest team in this section, where, some say, the more powerful cars can exceed 162mph (260km/h)!

The 550 Spyder finishes the 1954 Mille Miglia at Brescia, winning its class.

And finally, once again in Brescia, as we return to the starting point at 16:26, after 12hr 35min 44sec of an unforgettable race! Herrmann and Linge are tired but extremely happy with their performance in the 550 Spyder, which has been confirmed as winning its class, almost 20 minutes ahead of the OSCA of Cabianca. Some minutes later, this joy is even greater, as they learn that they have achieved a magnificent sixth place overall, holding their own against more powerful cars and proving the worth of the 550 Spyder and its recent new engine. Brilliant performance, unforgettable adventure ... that only a train could almost upset!

The victory in the Mille Miglia 1954 went to Alberto Ascari, the only survivor of the official Lancia team, completing the race in 11hr 26min 10sec at an average speed of 86.7mph (139.6km/h). Ferrari also only managed to take one of the factory cars back to Brescia, that of Vittorio Marzotto, which finished in second place. As usual, the extreme rigours of the race manifested in accidents and mechanical failures, which eliminated many of the competitors. Of the 374 who began the race in Brescia, only 180 finished.

In addition to the extraordinary performance of Herrmann–Linge and the 550,[12] Porsche also won the class GT–1.5-litres, with the 356 Super of von Frankenberg/Sauter. In Zuffenhausen, news of these successes

Porsche 550 Spyder of Herrmann/ Linge and 356 Super of von Frankenberg/ Sauter at the factory in Zuffenhausen after their superb performances at the 1954 Mille Miglia.

naturally brought great satisfaction and, a few days later, cars and drivers were greeted at the factory by Ferry Porsche and workers, who joined in the inner courtyard to congratulate them and others involved in the legendary Italian race.

Ferry Porsche (in the centre) congratulates the works teams, just arrived back from the 1954 Mille Miglia.

19–23 NOVEMBER 1954, TUXTLA, MEXICO

We are in the city of Tuxtla Gutiérrez, in southern Mexico near the border with Guatemala, almost at the start time of the largest automobile adventure on the American continent, the famous Carrera Panamericana. With a format very similar to the European Mille Miglia, the Mexican race is even tougher by virtue of its

Three Porsches at rest during the 1954 Carrera Panamericana (no.53 of Ernst Hirz, no.55 of Herrmann and no.58 of Segura/Linge).

duration, the type of roads used, the weather conditions and all kinds of incidents that the over-enthusiastic spectators can cause. The competition extends over 1,875 miles (3,000km) to Ciudad Juárez in the north, near the border with the US state of New Mexico, and is divided into eight challenging legs.

I am now 'inhabiting' a beautiful 550 Spyder, chassis no.04, which will be driven by the well-known and admired Hans Herrmann, who will race alone, without a co-driver, as the regulations allow. I am a little anxious, because this adventure will certainly be for me the hardest and most dangerous of all those I have lived up to now. In fact, instead of 'living' the event in a more or less calm situation, inside of a body panel or another component in aluminium, this time I could only find a 'ride' on an engine component, the now famous type 547, which uses that material in the crankcase, cylinder heads and other parts. This engine definitely abandons any component of VW origin and is considered a masterpiece of mechanical engineering, in which Porsche places high hopes. In its architecture, the four overhead camshafts stand out, moved through shafts with bevel gears from the crankshaft, a complex solution that demands manufacturing and assembly tolerances in the order of hundredths of a millimetre. In fact, its assembly is so laborious and delicate that it consumes at least 120 work hours by very experienced and skilled technicians.

So it will not be a quiet trip through the Mexican roads, as Herrmann will not fail to extract the most from the machine, whose power is greater than

110bhp at 7,800rpm. I can hardly imagine the noise, vibration and temperature in its interior. In each cylinder head there are four valves, driven by the shafts and gears, which will open and close 130 times every second in accordance with the movement of the pistons, whose maximum linear velocity inside the cylinder reaches 90ft/s (27m/s). The generated heat must be dissipated by the oil and the cooling fan, which will be competing with the torrid temperatures of the Mexican plains. Anyway, I predict many hours of physical suffering, but also of pure pleasure!

Of course, Herrmann will have little chance to fight for victory in the overall standing, since there are far more powerful cars competing, such as the Ferraris with V12 engines of 4.5-litre displacement, whose most famous drivers are Umberto Maglioli and Phil Hill. Also for the first time in this race are two British Austin Healeys, one of them driven by Carroll Shelby. The United States also has representatives from different automobile marques, betting on the power of their different V8 engines. In the Porsche factory team there are three cars – in addition to ours with the no.55, there are two other 550s, no.56 driven by Jaroslav Juhan, a Czech now living in Guatemala, and no.58, driven by the Argentine Fernando Segura. The Porsche 550s will have to face, in the struggle for victory in the 1500cc class, Borgwards and OSCAs, one of them driven by the famous Louis Chiron.

We are now about to leave for the first stage, which will take us to Oaxaca, a distance of 330 miles (528km). The crowd watching the start enthusiastically welcomes each competitor, as each one leaves at high speed towards the mountains, where we will have to travel on roads with very steep and difficult climbs.

Herbert Linge (centre) looks at the 550 Spyder of Hans Herrmann.

It's now our turn to start the Panamericana. Herrmann accelerates and departs confidently as the flag drops. The noise of the engine from the point where I am becomes overwhelming, but at the same time invigorating. Herrmann has to give his best, especially in the last 62 miles (100km) of the stage, trying to lose as little time as possible on the steep mountain paths, which clearly favour the more powerful cars. In this first stage the victory goes to the white Ferrari of Phil Hill, which travelled the 330 miles (528km) in 3hr 25min at an astonishing average speed of 96.8mph (154.9km/h). In the 1500cc class the best time is for a Borgward, with our fellow teammate Juhan finishing in second with a time of 3hr 45min, which corresponds to a significant average of 88mph (141km/h). Herrmann achieves fifth position, a little below his expectations, but it is only the first leg and many miles are still to come.

The second leg connects Oaxaca to Puebla, 256 miles (410km), where the main difficulty is crossing the Sierra Madre. Maglioli (Ferrari) wins the overall classification, Bechem (Borgward) repeats his victory in the class, with Juhan arriving in second place, while we come immediately afterwards.

In the third leg we have only 80 miles (128km) to Mexico City. The highest point of the stage is crossing the Llano Grande and Rio Frio at 10,826ft (3,248m) In these roads we improve a little, gaining second place in the stage, behind Chiron's OSCA.

The fourth stage takes the competitors to León, totalling 267 miles (427km). Many are forced to retire due to accidents caused by fog and very slippery roads, but for us everything goes well, and we win the class for the first time, followed by Juhan. In the class standings at the end of this leg, it is the two Porsches that are already in front, with Juhan leading. Among the most powerful cars is Maglioli (Ferrari), which now dominates the events.

The fifth leg between León and Durango is 333 miles (533km) long and allows high speeds along a flat course, being covered by the winner, Maglioli, at the fantastic average speed of 116mph (185.9km/h). Herrmann, winning our class, achieved a no less astonishing average of 105.6 mph (169.9km/h). It was a leg completed almost all the way at the maximum possibilities of the car, which becomes almost reckless when taking into account the speeds attained on what are still public roads. It was with some relief that I saw this stage coming to an end and that I could rest after 2hr 24min of high revs and strong emotions!

The sixth leg, consisting of 249 miles (401km) between Durango and Parral, is similar to the previous one regarding the speeds attained, and the results are also identical.

The seventh stage of 185 miles (297km) between Parral and Chihuahua gives us one more victory at an even more extraordinary average of 120.8mph (194.4km/h) (I am beginning to get familiar with these crazy speeds!) and we are now just twenty-four seconds behind Juhan. It goes without saying that the average speed performed by Maglioli was greater than ours – exactly

135.48mph (218km/h), which reinforces the idea of how fantastic and unique this race is!

We are now counting down to the end of this great adventure. The 550 has endured the effort well, also thanks to the performance of the mechanics, assisting it at the end of each stage. Many of the competitors have already retired, either because of breakdowns or accidents, leaving many cars and drivers stranded along the course.

Finally, we get to the last day of the event, with a 229-mile (368km) leg to Ciudad Juárez, which is practically a long straight, done with the 'pedal to the metal'. More than 100,000 spectators are waiting anxiously for the arrival of the competitors. With Ciudad Juárez already full of enthusiasts, thousands of cars have left the city to spread out with their occupants along the last 25 miles (40km) of the road that leads to the city. For us, this last leg is a constant duel with teammate Juhan, culminating in the arrival of the two 550s side by side (despite having started the stage one minute after him), to the great excitement of the cheering onlookers. So we finish this last leg at the extraordinary average of 116.2 mph (187km/h), confirming a class victory and a fantastic third place in the overall classification.

BELOW LEFT: **Hans Herrmann followed by Jaroslav Juhan near the finish line of the 1954 Carrera Panamericana ...**

It is our just reward for five days of gruelling competition against much more powerful machines, on difficult terrain and in a challenging environment, making this 'crazy' adventure all the more unforgettable!

BELOW RIGHT: **... which they finished side by side!**

The V Carrera Panamericana was won by Umberto Maglioli in a 4.9-litre Ferrari (at an average speed of 107.33mph (172.7km/h), but it was also an extraordinary event for Porsche, which, with its small 550s, managed to reach the third and fourth places, finishing amongst the four Ferraris in the top positions. Porsche and its drivers won even more admiration

Porsche team at the 1954 Carrera Panamericana. From left: Herbert Linge, Hans Herrmann, Huschke von Hanstein and Jaroslav Juhan.

from enthusiasts and fans through their performance in this race. The name 'Carrera' would become definitively linked to the more powerful models of the marque, such as the 356s equipped with the 547 Fuhrmann engine and later to the most powerful versions of 911s, or to top models, as the Carrera GT shown in 2000.

27 MAY 1956, NÜRBURGRING, GERMANY

It is almost 09:00, on a beautiful day and the Nürburgring's 1,000km race is about to start. This is the hardest and most merciless track of the Championship. The 14.3 miles (22.8km) and seventy curves do not forgive mistakes, as only the best win here. It is necessary that the start be this early, as the race will last almost 7 hours, to fulfil the foreseen forty-four laps.

Some of the best racing drivers currently are in attendance: Fangio; Moss; Phil Hill; Taruffi; Behra; Trintignant; Hawthorn; Collins; and Brooks. Naturally, they drive the most powerful cars – Ferraris, Maseratis, Aston Martins and Jaguars – and will all be fighting for victory in the overall standing. But the fight in the lower-displacement class will also be lively and that is the battle in which I will be involved. Porsche is taking part in the Sports/Racing Cars class of up to 1500cc with two works cars, the one in which I'm going to 'live' a few more thrilling hours, a 550 Spyder driven by Hans Herrmann/Richard von Frankenberg, and another for the Wolfgang von Trips/Umberto Maglioli team.

The small but fast 550 Spyder, with engines half the displacement of the fastest cars, attained quite interesting lap times in qualifying and dominated the class, with Herrmann achieving 10min 26sec. This was approximately 23 seconds slower than Fangio's Ferrari and even in front of the best Aston Martin. That gap represents 1sec per km, which showcases well the worth of Stuttgart's cars in the face of much more powerful opponents. Hence we are on the sixth position of the starting grid, Le Mans-style (with cars diagonally in sequence to each other on the side of the track, as is traditional in many endurance races) with our 'sister' car immediately after us.

Seventy thousand people will watch the race, filling the stands and other 'hotspots' around the circuit, with some strategically placed in the most unusual places, like the one I can see up on a lamp post and another one perching on a fence. Some of the drivers are perfectly relaxed, such as the British Stirling Moss and Mike Hawthorn, playing like two teenagers. Fangio is leaning on the fence and even Louis Chiron is sitting on the asphalt, waiting for the speaker to

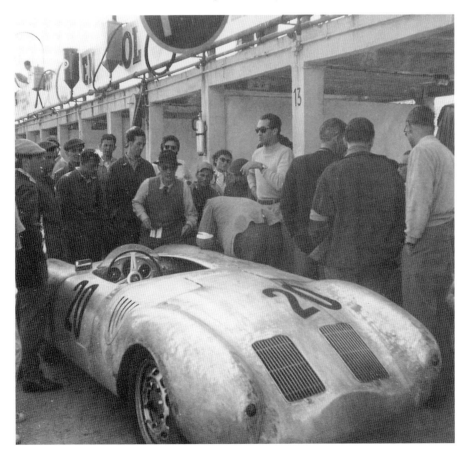

Porsche 550A of Herrmann/von Frankenberg at the pits of Nürburgring circuit (notice the unpainted aluminium body).

Hans Herrmann on the attack at the 1956 Nürburgring 1,000km.

announce 'Achtung, achtung, eine Minute!'.[13] At that time they all get ready for a short sprint. 'Fünf, vier, drei, zwei, eins ...'[14] and the flag is waved. I can see von Frankenberg running towards me, jumping behind the steering wheel and pressing the starter button, but the engine doesn't start ... another attempt and another, until finally we're off with the sound of screeching tyres.

I can see ahead of me that the fastest to get going are: Moss (Maserati); Hawthorn (Jaguar); Collins (Aston Martin); Alfonso de Portago (Ferrari); and Fangio (Ferrari). The rumble of the engines is huge and now passing the end of the start/finish straight towards the South corner, I can see the two 'climber' spectators falling to the ground at the same time, such was their excitement ... or the shockwave that hit them! Von Frankenberg is giving it his best to recover the seconds lost at the start. We have passed Hoheneichen and now we're reaching Flugplatz, where I always get that empty feeling, when the car almost lifts off the asphalt and the wheels are about to spin free, followed by the crunch when the suspension compresses a few metres further forwards. After that, we accelerate to the maximum until Aremberg. I feel the vigorous braking into this right-hand turn, then we go under the bridge and up towards Adenauer Forst, where the agility of the 550 is noticeable, by maintaining a perfect trajectory on this hard right–left–right.

The battle up ahead is close, since I can hear through the circuit's loud speakers who are the successive leaders on this first lap: Moss; Hawthorn; Fangio; and Moss again. We go into the famous Karussell and I feel the characteristic bumpiness of the inner lane, very slanted and with its surface made of concrete slabs.

We now go through the sinuous and demanding zone until the long Döttinger Höhe straight, where we can relax a bit. Soon we see the Continental tower of the start/finish straight and we complete the first lap of this long race. Von Trips in the other 550 went by in seventh position, but I can't work out right now what our position is, but that matters little at the moment, as Von Frankenberg is already accelerating towards the South corner, for another exciting lap to the Nordschleife!

On the third lap we pass Musso's Ferrari, which went off track and overturned, with the race marshals trying to flip the car back and free the driver. Later, on the fifth lap, we experience brake problems and von Frankenberg decides to stop in at the pits to have them checked. With this stop, we are overtaken by a rival in our class, Edgar Barth's AWE.

Hans Herrmann is now at the wheel and is committed to recovering lost time, by demanding the most from the car. Near the middle of the race, I hear through the loudspeakers that the Moss/Behra Jaguar has been forced to retire from the race with engine problems, putting Fangio/Castelotti's Ferrari in front. Despite the setbacks, halfway through the race with twenty-two laps completed, we are in seventh place, between the Aston Martins of Walker/Salvadori and Collins/Brooks. But we are only in the middle of this hard race and it would be good if we kept this place, along with the fact that von Trips/Maglioli are in a magnificent fifth place.

Hans Herrmann refuels the 550A at the Nürburgring 1,000km.

Out in front, the battle is still very close, especially because Maserati's sport manager has made his star drivers, Moss and Behra, after their retirement, go to the Taruffi/Shell car. Behra is now in second position and approaching the leaders. Our 550 Spyder continues at a constant pace, getting closer to the end of the race, which is now being led again by Moss, since Fangio was forced to stop to refuel.

We are now on the much awaited final lap, on which we find two of the cars that were racing in front of us stopped due to mechanical failures – Walker/ Salvadori's Aston Martin and Hawthorn/Titterington's Jaguar. Our enthusiasm and expectation increase, feeling great relief when we pass the chequered flag, after forty-four laps and over 8 hours of racing.

The final result is a 'tasty' sixth place. Herrmann and von Frankenberg are satisfied, but even more so are von Trips and Maglioli, who have taken the 550 to a wonderful fourth place and victory in the class, even though they did not have second gear available in the last few laps.

In a race as difficult as the Nürburgring's 1,000km, which is hard and demanding for both cars and drivers, two facts stand out:

- the extraordinary struggle for victory, in which the main players were Stirling Moss (the brilliant winner) and Juan Manuel Fangio
- the excellent performance of the Porsche 550s,[15] which were able to participate in a 'battle of giants' to the amazement of spectators and journalists. Cyril Posthumus, for example, wrote in the prestigious English weekly *Autosport* that the Stuttgart cars were 'indecently fast!'.

10 JUNE 1956, CIRCUITO DELLE MADONIE, SICILY

Two weeks after the 1,000km of Nürburgring, the oldest race in motor-sport history takes place, the Targa Florio, which has run in Sicily since 1906. This year it is the fiftieth anniversary of this tough race, whose 44.7-mile (72km) circuit uses winding public roads in the north of the island. It is a very demanding race, not only due to the difficult and tricky roads, but also because of its length, ten laps totalling 447 miles (720km), with 800 curves in every lap. The cars suffer with the poor road conditions in some areas and the high temperatures, plus there are also several imponderable factors (public, animals, accidents) that may jeopardize in a moment the aspirations of competitors.

Porsche was not intending to participate in this race, but the good results obtained at the Nürburgring, plus some pressure from enthusiasts of the marque on Huschke von Hanstein, the racing director, led him to enrol almost at the last minute. So it has been possible only to provide a 550A and two mechanics for the great challenge. The drivers enrolled are von Hanstein himself and

Umberto Maglioli. Hanstein has put his name down as a possible driver just in case, because the idea is that Maglioli, one of the most experienced drivers in this event (and winner in 1953), will do the whole race himself, which is allowed by regulations.

While the car was being prepared in Zuffenhausen I managed to 'infiltrate' it, because I did not want to lose the chance to experience such a prestigious race. In this event there is no official practice, due to the difficulty in closing the public roads on which the race takes place. However, many of the drivers risk making some laps around the circuit beforehand, with all kinds of mobile or fixed obstacles to test their dexterity (and luck!), crossing villages (Cerda, Caltavuturo, Campofelice) and overcoming the difficult and narrow mountain roads, with tight corners and no visibility.

I am now in a garage in Palermo, 25 miles (40km) away from the circuit. Maglioli and von Hanstein have brushes and buckets of white paint in their hands and I realize suddenly that they are in the process of giving the 550 a paint job,[16] though I cannot understand the reason why! After finishing the white coat, they then add the colours of the Italian flag. It might be a ploy to secure the support of the Sicilian public!

On the day of the race, the start is given early, because the fifty-six cars leave one by one, every 30 seconds. The main candidates for victory this year are, at least theoretically, Ferrari with three works cars, Maserati (one works car and three more private) and Mercedes (winner in the previous year) with three semi-official cars. These are the 'Goliaths', for whom the small 'Davids' (Porsche and OSCA) will try to make life difficult.

Umberto Maglioli gets ready for the start of 1956 Targa Florio.

At the expected time, when the start flag is shown to us, Maglioli departs, set on making a great race, and we begin to move quickly through the winding road up towards Cerda. Maglioli will attempt the feat of doing all the race alone, which regardless of the result will nonetheless be a great sports achievement, because the event will last more than 7 hours under very difficult conditions. I don't know if Maglioli believes he has a chance of an overall win, but he is certainly determined to give it his best shot. And indeed he has to, because not only are the most powerful cars hard to beat, but even the little OSCA (which beat the Porsches in the last Mille Miglia) may prove to be a difficult opponent.

The small white 550 has completed the first lap at a good pace and we have already passed through Cerda and Caltavuturo, with a very enthusiastic crowd cheering us on. We are now in the mountainous roads towards Collesano, starting the descent towards the sea and Campofelice, after which, in the last part of the circuit, there is a long 3.7-mile (6km) straight, which provides some respite, but then we go back to the normal pace, with a rapid succession of curves to the finish line.

At the end of the first lap the Ferrari of Eugenio Castellotti is in first position and, to the astonishment of many, the OSCA of Giulio Cabianca follows it with a 2min 36sec delay, and we come 7 seconds behind in third. Not bad for a start, but nine laps of struggle and suffering remain and no one is willing to relax the pressure. In this first lap, the 300SL of von Trips and one of the Maseratis have already retired, while Olivier Gendebien (Ferrari) lost 15 minutes when he went off the road.

On the second lap, Castellottti is forced to retire with a broken drive shaft on his Ferrari. On this lap, we have passed the OSCA of Cabianca, so we are in the lead! This position is somewhat unexpected, at least at such an early stage of the race; Maglioli is now extremely excited and even more set on winning again in Sicily. Seventeen seconds behind our 550 no.84 come Cabianca and Piero Taruffi (Maserati). In the following laps, Maglioli manages both to maintain the leadership and to increase our advantage. In the sixth lap, he makes his only stop at the pits in Cerda for refuelling. At this point, our lead over Cabianca is already greater than 5 minutes.

Umberto Maglioli waits for the departure signal of what should be a fantastic race and victory.

Maglioli impresses by the speed and smoothness of his driving, accompanied by the good performance of the 550, which proves itself to be perfectly capable of meeting the exacting demands of both driver and race. The laps follow one another, with Maglioli showing an undeniable champion's class and an impressive resistance to fatigue that is certainly within the reach of only a few.

As we approach the finish line at the end of the tenth and final lap, fireworks are launched to warn the public of our approach. To us, they already sound like a celebration, because Cabianca is almost 13 minutes behind and it is with great joy that we pass the chequered flag at the end, 7hr 54min into the race. Von Hanstein comes to us and warmly welcomes Maglioli, delighted with this extraordinary victory and what it means for the brand. The last-minute bet has proved to be a winning one!

This victory in the prestigious Targa Florio confirmed the quality of Porsche as a competitive car manufacturer for endurance events, validating at the same time the concept that light and agile cars with small displacement engines can win against much more powerful and expensive cars. This victory was really important for Porsche, as it was its first overall win in a major endurance sports car race, beginning a very successful history in this motor-sport category. It was also the first victory in an event that became charismatic for Porsche and where it managed a total of eleven victories until 1973, the last year in which the race counted towards the World Championship. The importance and significance of this event for the brand became so relevant that in 1965 the 'open' variant of the 911 was named the 'Targa', in honour of the achievements attained on the legendary Sicilian circuit.

The 550A Spyder of Umberto Maglioli, already the race leader, is refuelled on the sixth lap.

CHAPTER FOUR

NEW CHALLENGES WITH NEW CARS: THE 1960s

26 MARCH 1960, SEBRING, USA

The sixty-five cars that have qualified for the 12 Hours of Sebring are lined up for a Le Mans-style start. It is almost 10:00 and there is a great bustle in this 'improvised' circuit, which uses the runways of an airbase and its access roads, totalling 5.2 miles (8.36km). This 12-hour race was first run in 1952 and in a few years has come to be one of the most well-known endurance races. With its long straights, the circuit clearly favours the more powerful cars and these have domi-nated the event in the last few years, but Porsche, refusing to be intimidated, has been participating with its small 550 and 718, but until now has only obtained class victories. In 1959, Wolfgang von Trips and Joakim Bonnier came in third place in the general standings in a 718 RSK.

Porsche 718 RS 60 of Hans Herrmann/ Olivier Gendebien with mechanic Eberhard Storz.

This year, Porsche is again trying to crash the party for the Ferraris and Maseratis equipped with powerful 3-litre engines and naturally the favourites to win. Porsche is counting on its 'armada' of five 718s, now type RS 60, which have few differences from the RSK used in 1959. There are two factory cars, even though they were enrolled by Jo Bonnier,[17] one (no.43) driven by himself and Graham Hill, and another (no.42) for Olivier Gendebien and Hans Herrmann. That is how I come now to be on no.42 chassis, in which Herrmann will set off for the long 12 hours of racing, wishing to win the already famous race in the land of 'Uncle Sam'!

There are, in fact, some interesting particularities on this side of the Atlantic, such as the fact that the starting grid is not formed in accordance to the times registered in the qualifying sessions, but instead in decreasing order of engine displacement of the competing cars. That is why we are well beyond the middle of the pack lined up for the start, according to our small 1600cc engines. Out in front are the Chevrolet Corvettes with their 5-litre engines, followed by the Ferraris and the Maseratis with 3-litre engines. The favourites to win are no doubt the Maserati 'Birdcage' Type 61s, with three cars and two very strong teams, the no.22 car with Carroll Shelby and Masten Gregory and the no.23 car with Stirling Moss and Dan Gurney.

Herrmann is now ready for the run to the 718 on the other side of the track as soon as the flag comes down, but he is also aware of how difficult it will be to reach victory with the Porsches (here nicknamed 'pygmies'). At 10:00 on the dot, the race is started; Herrmann crosses the track and jumps into the 718 and gets going quickly. I immediately feel the irregular bumps caused by the joints on the track between the cement slabs, which are characteristic of this circuit laid out on an airbase. Herrmann does not start completely on the attack because he knows that the race is long and hard and that mechanical endurance is fundamental to achieving a good result.

In the first laps we are staying below tenth place. Ahead of us, Stirling Moss in the Maserati is on the attack, after having trouble starting the engine, but he has four Ferraris in front of him, with Pete Lovely in the lead. The first lap is somewhat confusing due to the peculiar order of the starting grid and there are already some cars in difficulty, like Bob Holbert, driving one of the three privately owned 718s in the competition, who has crashed into one of the haybales on the side of the track. Moss is still unstoppable, as at the end of the second lap he only has Lovely's Ferrari in front of him; by the third lap he's in the lead. Jo Bonnier, with a fantastic start, manages to get into fifth place behind the Ferrari of the young Rodriguez brothers.

The steady pace that Herrmann has been setting is meanwhile interrupted, due to the rear brakes starting to lock up, so he decides to call into the pits to obtain mechanical assistance. While that happens, one of the favourite Maseratis, driven by Shelby/Gregory, is forced to retire due to engine problems, but

Hans Herrmann drives the 718 RS 60 to the first overall victory for Porsche in the 12 Hours of Sebring (1960).

in front of us there are still two cars of the Italian brand, with Moss in front of Walt Hansgen.

After almost 2 hours of racing, the stops in the pits for exchanging drivers start to happen and Herrmann hands the car over to Gendebien in seventh position, with thirty-three laps completed. This is the same number as the 'sister' car in which Graham Hill now replaces Bonnier, at fourth position in the general standings. In front it is still Moss/Gurney's Maserati, with thirty-five laps. The no.44 718 of Bob Holbert, Roy Schechter and Howard Fowler is now even further behind since it ran out of fuel on the hairpin, the slowest turn of the circuit.

The heat can now clearly be felt and it affects the drivers as well as the mechanical parts and tyres of the cars. At 14:00, after 4 hours of racing, we're in fifth position right behind no.43 718, with one fewer lap. But there are still 8 hours of racing to go and anything can happen. As proof of that, we now find Bonnier/Hill's 718 stopped at the Webster turn, forced to retire with engine problems. Is the same going to happen to us? That fear is slightly overcome when, within a short amount of time, the Ferrari of Daigh/Ginther, which was in second place, also retires with engine problems. All of a sudden, we are in third place behind Moss's Maserati and the Ferrari of the Rodriguez brothers. The enthusiasm of the team is clear when we go into the pits for another driver exchange.

When it's almost 18:00, Moss stops in the pits to uncover the headlights, since the night is quickly approaching. Our distance to the leader diminishes and the expectation level increases. Herrmann pushes a bit harder and suddenly, after a few laps, we unexpectedly see Moss's Maserati going towards the pit lane again (with gearbox problems), from which it does not reappear. The second place is ours! Anything seems possible now, but could this be too much optimism?

But it seems that the gods are truly with us when we hear the announcement through the circuit's speakers that the no.28 Ferrari has just retired with clutch problems. Herrmann and Gendebien can hardly believe that they are now the race leaders, having driven 148 laps until 19:00, and having also a 4-lap lead over the 718 of Holbert/Schechter/Fowler, which has made a good recovery. In third place is the Maserati of Dave Causey and Luke Stear, seven laps behind. The favourite teams are all out of the race, or out of the fight for the win! However, one must stay calm, since there are still 3 hours until the end of the race and nothing is assured.

Thankfully, everything goes well in these last hours, with Herrmann and Gendebien taking the 718 without any problems to the finish line, where the photographers are fighting for a good viewpoint from which to record the surprise victory of a 'small' Porsche. The no.42 718 has completed 196 laps, having driven 1,014 miles (1,632km) at an average speed of 84.93mph (136.6km/h). The story of David and Goliath has once again been retold and the joy among the Porsche team is enormous. It is a resounding victory: two Porsches in the two first places followed by five Ferraris! When the phone rings in Zuffenhausen to give the good news, there will certainly be a lot of rejoicing over this brilliant victory.

The 718 started its career in 1957, as an evolution of the 550A. It was projected with more fluid and aerodynamic lines, also with improvements to the chassis, which became lighter but also more resistant. To make the car's front part as thin as possible, Porsche developed an innovative system for cooling the engine oil that consisted of a bent line of tubing fixed on the inside of the front hood, avoiding in this way the use of a radiator, which would require the intake of air, always detrimental to aerodynamics and drag. The headlights were installed behind transparent plastic covers that perfectly followed the bodywork's profile. The suspension was also redesigned to make it more efficient under stress and also to allow for the decrease of the height of the 718. Initially, the

Wolfgang von Trips won the first European Hill Climb Championship for Porsche in 1958. (Here racing at Gaisberg on the way to victory.)

engine fitted was the 547 Fuhrmann of 1500cc and 135bhp that was already used in the 550A. The car was 44.4lb (20kg) lighter than its predecessor.

In the first year the 718 did not gain any outstanding results, but in 1958, with some improvements to the suspension and engine, it achieved victory in its class and third place in the overall standing at the 24 Hours of Le Mans, with Jean Behra and Hans Herrmann, and second place in the Targa Florio with Behra and Giorgio Scarlatti.

In 1959, with some more changes to the suspension and engine (which was now producing 148bhp), it achieved victory in the Targa Florio with Edgar Barth and Wolfgang Seidl, jumping for the first time into the roll of Porsche's most prestigious victories. During 1958 and 1959, the 718 also competed successfully in many races of the European Hill Climb Championship, where its lightness and manoeuvrability worked their charm. Thus Wolfgang von Trips in 1958 and Edgar Barth in 1959 were crowned European champions with relative ease, another important contribution to the brand's racing history.

In 1960 the 718 underwent some more changes, the biggest one being the height of the windshield as a result of new regulations, and the car became known as RS 60 instead of RSK. The cockpit was now wider too and had larger doors. It could be equipped with two types of engines, the 547/3 of 1488cc and 150bhp, and the 547/4 of 1587cc and 160bhp. Besides the victory in the 12 Hours of Sebring, Porsche gained in 1960 another beautiful victory in the Targa Florio with Jo Bonnier and Hans Herrmann.

In 1961, the RS61 came along with changes to the bodywork, even racing a 'coupé' variant but without a 'roof' in the 24 Hours of Le Mans, where the Gregory/Holbert team won the class and achieved fifth place in the general standings. This car used a type 587 engine with 1996cc and 185bhp. The 718 GTR ('coupé') still gained a third win in 1963 for this model in the Targa Florio, with Jo Bonnier and Carlo Abate.

The bodywork of this 'coupé' mounted on the no.47 chassis would evolve into a beautiful Spyder called W-RS, which, with an increase in the distance between axles to 2,300mm, would come to allow for the use in 1962 of a type 771 8-cylinder engine, with 2-litres and 210bhp. This was an evolution of the 753 Formula One engine installed in the 804. With this engine, the car would get the victory in its class and an eighth place in the general standings in the 1962 24 Hours of Le Mans, with Edgar Barth[18] and Herbert Linge.

The 718 W-RS remained competitive for many years, with victories both in circuits and hill climbing races, where it won the title of European Hill Climbing Champion in 1963 and 1964 with Edgar Barth at the wheel. Due to its long sporting career, the W-RS with the no.047 chassis would come to bear the endearing nickname of *Großmutter.*[19]

The 718 also competed in 1958 in Formula Two races, as an altered version with a central single-seat cockpit. There were victories in Reims and Avus, with Jean Behra at the wheel. At the end of 1959, 'open-wheel' versions were built with the same purpose and these had the designation of F2-718 or 718-2. The first great victory came in 1960 at Aintree with Stirling Moss, immediately followed by Jo Bonnier and Graham Hill in

TOP LEFT: **Edgar Barth in the 718 W-RS** *Großmutter* **at Cesana-Sestrières Hill Climb (1964).**

TOP RIGHT: **Edgar Barth ready to start the Cesana-Sestrières Hill Climb (1964).**

RIGHT: **Edgar Barth in the 718 W-RS starts the 1964 Cesana-Sestrières Hill Climb on his way to victory.**

the other two identical 718-2s that Porsche had signed up for the event. Bonnier also won the Nürburgring F2 Grand Prix. Moss, Bonnier and Herrmann won another four races before the end of the season, taking Porsche to victory in the World Formula Two Championship.

In 1961, with the changes in the Formula One regulations, in which the maximum engine size was decreased to 1500cc, the 718-2s were now able to compete in the premium class. Of course, the power (180bhp) of their engines limited greatly their aspirations, but even so Dan Gurney achieved a fourth place at the end of the Championship, with his best results being obtained in the French, Italian and United States Grand Prixs, in all of which he finished second. Jo Bonnier also obtained some results, having been close to victory also in the French Grand Prix, in which he vied with Giancarlo Baghetti's Ferrari in the last few laps, before having to retire with engine problems.

The experience obtained with the 718-2 would come to be used in the development of the first true Formula One car made by Porsche, the 804, which would compete in the World Championship in 1962.

8 JULY 1962, ROUEN, FRANCE

The French Formula One Grand Prix is the fourth race of the 1962 World Championship and is being run at the Rouen-Les-Essarts circuit. It is a warm summer day and there are 80,000 spectators longing to see a showdown among the best drivers. Dan Gurney is revving up the 8-cylinder engine of the 804 while he waits for the flag to come down. We are on the third row of the grid and Dan Gurney can see the Lola-Climax of John Surtees and Jack Brabham in front of him. A few metres ahead on the first row are the Cooper-Climax of Bruce McLaren, the BRM of Graham Hill and the Lotus 25 of Jim Clark. Dan Gurney knows that his chances of winning are not the greatest, but he is willing to give it all he can and do his best.

The starter lowers the flag and the cars dart off quickly towards the first corner of this hard and demanding track. We hold our position while out in front Graham Hill takes the lead, followed by John Surtees. Dan Gurney is now defending his position from Masten Gregory (Lotus-BRM), the Porsche flat-8 (type 753) is revving almost constantly between 8,000 and 10,000rpm and screaming right at Gurney's back with its air intakes and the cooling fan only a few centimetres away from his head. Gurney drives with his habitual coldness, drawing the trajectories millimetrically, with his penetrating gaze anticipating the approach of each turn.

On the tenth lap, Bruce McLaren and Jack Brabham, who have been in front of us, retire from the race, the first one due to a crash and the second one with suspension problems. That has moved us into fourth place, which a few laps later becomes third, when Surtees withdraws with engine problems on his Lola-Climax. Thus in the middle of the race we are behind Clark and Hill, who are battling each other for first position. Gurney continues at a fast and regular pace, when suddenly the excitement increases as we pass Clark, who has been forced to retire with steering problems. Gurney believes that it might still be his day and is getting all he can out of the 804, which continues to work perfectly. And suddenly, in the last third of the race, Hill also has injection problems in the engine of his BRM and is forced to withdraw.

It is with great excitement that as Gurney enters the start/finish straight on the fifty-fourth lap he sees the panel held by one of his mechanics to let him know that he is in the lead of the race! From there until the chequered flag Gurney is taking care of his 804 as best he can, so that he might make history for the Stuttgart marque. And so it happens, as we cross the finish line on the fifty-fourth

Dan Gurney in the 804 at the 1962 French Grand Prix.

Dan Gurney drives the 804 faultlessly to victory at the Formula One 1962 France Grand Prix at Rouen.

lap, Porsche wins its first Formula One race. Gurney is overjoyed both to achieve this honour for the marque and also to take the highest step on the podium for the first time in a race for the Formula One World Drivers' Championship.

This victory was just reward for all the effort that Porsche had been making over the last two years, in this new challenge that was Formula One. The Stuttgart brand had decided on this incursion into the most prestigious automotive sport championship in 1961 with the change in the regulations that limited the displacement of engines to 1.5-litres and the minimum weight to 993lb (450kg) These regulations were in sympathy with the brand's core philosophy for developing its competition cars: lightweight and small, but with powerful engines.

For the 1962 Championship, Porsche decided to raise its bet, building an entirely new car, the 804, with a new 8-cylinder engine, type 753, which delivered 180bhp at 9,200rpm. With this power it was possible to do battle with the English cars (Lotus, Brabham, BRM), whose power was similar. Although the victory in the French Grand Prix turned out to be the only one in Championship races, a third place in the German Grand Prix was obtained and Gurney finished fifth in the Championship. Meanwhile, the 804 (also with Gurney) achieved a beautiful victory at the 'homemade' circuit of Solitude in a race outside of the Championship.

After analysing everything at the end of the season, Ferry Porsche decided not to continue with the Formula One project, because he considered that the costs were too high and the technical solutions would be too difficult to apply to series production cars. So Porsche returned to its origins and would again centre its attention on the development of cars for competing in endurance races on circuits and on the open road, in which it had already obtained significant and important victories.

12 SEPTEMBER 1963, FRANKFURT

After Dan Gurney's win in the French Formula One Grand Prix, I returned to the factory in Zuffenhausen, where for a long time people had been talking about the car that would replace the 356. At this time, both the engine and the bodywork were in full development. The main person in charge of the engine was Hans Mezger, who had collaborated in the building of the 8-cylinder type 753, which equipped the 804. Working together with Ferdinand Piëch, the flat-6 (901/01) started to take shape, at the same time that the bodywork, which was initially the responsibility of Erwin Komenda, was also getting closer to its definitive shape under the guidance of 'Butzi' Porsche, Ferry's oldest son.

Excited by the frantic environment accompanying the development of the car, I stayed around the offices and workshops where the first prototypes of the 901, the number that had been given to this ambitious project, were born. The initial directives that Ferry Porsche had established were aimed at getting a car that would be slightly bigger than the 356, with more space for its passengers and baggage. It should be able to accommodate a golfbag in its boot and be more powerful, while maintaining the 'family look' of its successful predecessor.

The first design that came from 'Butzi''s drawing table in 1959, which became known as type 754 or T7, was a four-seater car, thanks to a wheelbase that was 1ft (30cm) bigger than the 356. A prototype was built at Reutter, but Ferry Porsche thought that its dimensions were too big for it to be considered a sports car. He therefore decided to relinquish having so much space for the passengers and asked the team to devise a compromise between space/dimensions, while also incorporating more of the design of the 356, mainly through a 'fastback' style rear.

Butzi went back to work, always staying loyal to the maxim from the Bauhaus school – 'Form follows function'. The wheelbase was reduced, the roof was short-ened and in this way the 'fastback' rear in the style of the 356 came around.

These were lively times in the project offices, with much heated debate about the changes that had been asked for. Erwin Komenda, who had overall responsibility for the project and had defended the larger dimension car, had a hard time accepting the guidance from Ferry Porsche, even though Butzi also agreed with it.

The development of the engine also wasn't easy and Hans Mezger had to dedicate himself fully to get to a final result in which the flat-6 engine with 2000cc put out 130bhp, which was considered enough for the desired objectives. One of the main guidelines by Ferry Porsche had been satisfied by getting a greater power than that of the Fuhrmann engine that equipped the Carrera models of the 356, but with a simpler and cheaper engine that in terms of maintenance was within reach of any mechanic with proper training. Besides its amazing performances both in power and consumption, the 901 engine had also been designed to be used as the basis for competition variants, with Mezger taking care to make it possible to increase the engine displacement in the future up to 3,000cc. Thirteen prototypes of the new car were built and thoroughly tested in 1962 and 1963.

And finally the big day of the presentation for the (almost) finished product to the public arrived, at the Frankfurt Auto Show, which opened its doors on 12 September 1963. It is here that I remember the path that took us to the presentation of the new model on which the brand now rests its best hopes. The Porsche stand isn't very big, but from the 901, painted in Light Yellow, I can see several units of the 356 that the brand brought to the show: an SC coupé in Togo Brown; a Carrera coupé in Signal Red; and a C cabriolet in Sky Blue.

The public starts to fill the venue of the Auto Show and the Porsche stand is quickly surrounded by people interested in seeing the new car, its characteristics and price. The reactions are diverse, from those who consider it to be too different from its predecessor, to those that give it unconditional praise. The 901 quickly becomes the star of the Auto Show, despite its series production being far from starting.

The 901 (later renamed 911) was one of the stars of the exhibition, with many people seeking information about the new Porsche, successor of the 356.

The days spent at the Frankfurt Auto Show were almost like a quiet 'holiday', far from the excitement of the races or the factory, but I really enjoyed taking part in the first steps of the 901 (or 911, I should say), which I bet will make history in the industry and automotive sport!

The car that Porsche presented in Frankfurt in 1963, which would come to be known as the 911 and not the 901,[20] would eventually reveal itself to be an extraordinary success throughout decades, becoming the 'icon' for the brand, inspiring and influencing the development and sales strategy of

The 901 engine was still under development when the car had its world debut at Frankfurt. The photo shows what seems to be a 'mock-up', or an experimental version of the future famous flat-6.

the new models throughout the coming years. Its lines became timeless and Butzi Porsche was forever connected to the brand created by his grandfather by his definitive contribution to this design and project. In fact, his passage through the design department, even though it was relatively short,[21] was striking for the creation of what are presumably the two most beautiful models in the brand's history, the 904 and the 911.

25 JANUARY 1965, MONTE CARLO, MONACO

After a week with a lot of cold and snow, the sunshine warming up the plaza in front of the palace is gratefully received by all those who are waiting for the start of the ceremony where the prizes for the thirty-fourth Monte Carlo Rally are going

The 911 begins its motorsport career at the 1965 Monte Carlo rally with Herbert Linge and Peter Falk.

A lot of snow and bad weather did not prevent a very good performance by the Porsche 911 team, who managed to get a promising fifth place in the overall classification of the Monégasque rally.

to be awarded. Herbert Linge and Peter Falk are by the sides of the red 911 in which they finished the Monégasque race in a worthy fifth place.

The successor of the 356 lived up to the first sporting event in which it partici-pated and I'm also particularly happy at being able to 'live' this adventure in the world's most famous rally. I had wanted to do it before, but had never found a good chance to 'get into' a participating team. But at the end of 1964 this wish became possible when Huschke von Hanstein decided to enrol the 911. I was excited, even though it was clear that Porsche would not fight for victory. It was basically a first racing experience for the 'newborn' 911, to test its capabilities and introduce it to the general public and to potential clients.

In fact, the enrolled car was nearly still a series one, since the changes done to it were few: a slight increase in power from 130 to 140/150bhp by using Weber carburettors instead of the Solex ones; the installation of 'navigation' equipment (two chronometers and a 'tripmaster') on the dashboard; and the addition of two supplementary headlights on the front hood and a rotating light mounted on the roof (that could be oriented from the inside, to improve lighting the road signs and crossroads). Also installed were a roll bar inside and a bar on the rear bumper, which, together with two leather straps on the sides of the engine cool-ing grid, allowed the navigator to put weight on the rear axle to help free the car if it got 'stuck' in the snow that was so frequent at this time of year on the Alpine roads where the rally takes place.

And in fact the snow was not lacking in this rally, especially during the Concen-tration Run. It was such a storm that it decimated a large part of the 237 contest-ants, as only 43 were able to get to the Principality before the start of the common route. They were really difficult conditions, but Linge, Falk and the 911 were able to overcome them to achieve good results. In the first special stage of 30.45 miles (49km), we completed it with a time of 52min 40sec, actually a bit faster than the 904 of the Eugen Böhringer/Rolf Wütherich team, which finished it in 52min 55sec. This team, which was also supported by the factory, would naturally be faster than ours, even though the 904 did not appear to be the ideal car for the conditions in which the rally was being driven. It was clear that the fight for the win would be between the small English Minis, which had won in 1964, and the Saabs, the Swedish cars with which Eric Carlsson won the first special stage.

It has been a revelation to see how the talented Linge, supported by Falk, kept overcoming the difficulties of the five special stages completed before arriving in Monte Carlo. Before the well-deserved night's rest, it is comforting to know that we are in an unexpected eighth place among the thirty-five admitted to the last leg of the rally. In the lead is Timo Mäkinen in one of the Minis, followed by a spectacular Lucien Bianchi in a Citroën DS 19. Also worth noting is the fourth place occupied by the Porsche 904 of Böhringer/Wütherich.

With our strength revived and motivated by the good initial result, Linge and Falk have settled into the 911 again, getting ready for the start of the Monaco–Monaco route, and it is with great satisfaction that I feel the flat-6 working again, with its characteristic 'growl', which allows the temperature to increase quickly, lessening the discomfort of the long and freezing night spent in the parc fermé with the other cars, next to the water of Monte Carlo Bay.

There has been a minor setback for Linge and Falk, when the studded tyres that they were counting on for this last stage were given to the 904 team which, with their great performance so far, justified that decision. The snow tyres are an important asset in the extremely difficult conditions that the rally has been driven in so far. Despite this misfortune, we set off towards the Alps for another six special stages, amongst them the famous and feared passage through the Turini!

Right after the start, we pass the Mini of Paddy Hopkirk/Henry Liddon, which has stopped so that its mechanics can weld a broken suspension. The conditions are difficult because the roads have quite a bit of snow and ice on them, which makes it a challenge to maintain the average speed of 37.3mph (60km/h) required in the connection routes between the special stages. It is impressive that there are still a few competitors without penalties, amongst them Böhringer and Wütherich in the 904.

Finally we have arrived to the start of the Turini. Herbert Linge, with fast but safe driving, has managed to put us in a spectacular third place in this special stage, with a time of 25min 31sec, right after Timo Mäkinen and Paul Easter (24min 39sec) and Böhringer/Wütherich (24min 47sec). The 911 is starting to get noticed and turning into an excellent rally car! The night is long, with four more special stages and also the demanding connection routes.

But everything goes well in this competition debut for the 911 and we arrive at Monte Carlo in a magnificent fifth place in the general standings. We are

also very happy because Böhringer and Wütherich in the 904 have finished in a spectacular second place, which is quite remarkable for a car (theoretically) much more suitable for track races. All that is left to do is to receive the prizes in the ceremony that is about to begin and then return to Zuffenhausen with the satisfaction of a job well done.

Porsches 904 (Eugen Böhringer/Rolf Wütherich) and 911 (Herbert Linge/Peter Falk) after receiving their trophies in the 1965 Monte Carlo rally.

The Porsche 911 that made its debut in rally racing in the prestigious Monte Carlo would become a recurrent and successful rally car in many countries and championships in the hands of both famous and almost unknown drivers. Its performance and endurance led to many victories in the following years and even produced Porsche European Rally Championship titles in 1967 (Sobiesław Zasada and Vic Elford) and 1968 (Pauli Toivonen). The 911 would win the Monte Carlo Rally four times: in 1968 with Vic Elford/David Stone, in 1969 and 1970 with Björn Waldegård/Lars Helmer and in 1978 with Jean-Pierre Nicolas/Vincent Laverne.

30 OCTOBER–4 NOVEMBER 1967, MONZA, ITALY

The engine that was just installed in the 911 R starts, letting out its 'growl' and making the glass of the windows in the workshop vibrate, as the mechanic revs it up to check that everything is in order. It's past midnight in Zuffenhausen, but strangely there are several mechanics still bustling round the car. It seems to be an emergency, since everyone is trying to complete their tasks quickly so that the car can depart to its destination.

Since my last adventure in a 911 (the Monte Carlo Rally in 1965), which was in fact its first participation in sporting events, I've been accompanying its development in the competition department and as soon as the opportunity came around I 'settled' in the first series production 911 R, expecting to enjoy thrilling moments on the track or on winding rally roads.

The interest in the 911 R is perfectly justified since this project has resulted in a profound change to the series 911, reducing its weight substantially while also drastically increasing the engine's power. The engine that was just installed is a variant of the one used in the 906, putting out 210bhp. Excited with the specifications of the new machine, I couldn't wait to go into action, but I didn't expect the opportunity to come so early.

The other 911 R being prepared in the workshop is also ready to go. I can see the driver, with road maps in his hands, settling in, fastening his seat belt and driving off quickly. One hour later it's our turn and I realize the one sitting behind the wheel is my previous acquaintance, Peter Falk, and through his conversation with the mechanics I realize that we are headed to Monza in Italy. Apparently we are going to participate in an attempt to establish several speed records at the Italian track. In front of us there are 311 miles (500km) of winding roads over the Alps and it seems that Peter Falk is interested in getting there as quickly as possible, testing the 911 R. It will be fun for sure!

The trip thankfully goes without incident and we arrive at the Monza circuit in the middle of the afternoon. In the pit, I can see that there is already a support zone prepared, where a 906 and the other 911 R, which left before us from Zuffenhausen, are stopped. The mechanics are around this 911 R and to my astonishment they start pulling it apart – shock absorbers, brakes, distributors, coils and so on – then put them in our car!

The Porsche 911 R is ready to attack (and beat) twelve speed records at the Monza circuit.

A quick pit stop to swap drivers and check the car's condition.

A little while after that, one of the drivers, who had started an attempt to establish the records in the 906, gets into my car and darts off quickly. I realize that at the end of the pit lane instead of going straight we turn right, entering the slanted speed ring. The 911 R quickly reaches its maximum speed with the left-side suspension 'smashed' against the hard pavement of the circuit. After a few laps at full speed we return to the pits, where from what the driver, the time officials and Peter Falk say, everything seems to be okay to start the marathon session to attempt to beat several world and international records. If everything goes well, it will consist of 96 hours (four days) always at full speed, hoping that the mechanical parts don't break! In terms of driving it might become a bit monotonous, but the challenge of the records will no doubt create a thrilling environment with great expectations.

Close to 20:00, everything is ready for the first driver to start this great marathon. At the exact hour, the time officials start their chronometers and Peter Falk gives the order to go. The total perimeter of the speed ring is 2.64 miles (4.25km) and everyone expects the 911 R to go around it quickly and many, many times!

With the first hours completed, the 911 R is rolling without problems, only stopping to refuel, clean the windshield and check the oil level. Meanwhile, the rain that is starting to fall makes the driver's job harder, but he continues to keep his 'pedal to the metal' regardless, getting the most out of this magnificent car. The sound of the engine, almost at maximum revs, invades the cabin, overpowering nearly all other sounds and giving expression to what is being demanded from the car. For those following the pace of the 911 R from the outside it is no doubt music to their ears, hoping to continue to hear its powerful 'growl' for many more hours.

The 911 R at full speed on the Monza banking. Notice the deformed plastic hood, which could not cope with the aerodynamic forces involved.

At 23:45 the tyres are replaced for the first time. During the stop we hear that the current average is around 129.27 mph (208km/h).

At 03:00, a slight sound of alarm: it is necessary to weld the driver's seat, which has come loose. But it is a quick action, little more than a minute, and off we go again, confident and wishing to get more miles done! At 08:00, with 12 hours passed, the average is getting close to 131.13mph (211km/h). Everything is going as planned and the drivers are taking turns, giving it their best and taking care of the mechanical parts the best they can.

The biggest difficulty for the drivers has been to deal with the weather conditions, including heavy rain and fog. The tyre supplier has run out of 'wet' tyres, forcing the use of slick tyres, on which grooves have been made manually to help drain water.

The hours pass and several records are successively beaten. Besides the normal periodic tyre replacements, it has only been necessary to replace the shock absorbers and the spark plugs. The 911 R, besides being quick, is demonstrating notable mechanical endurance!

After one more stint, the 911 R comes to the pits for refuelling and eventually a change of driver and tyres.

And finally comes the last day, the longest for the drivers and the team, who are all showing the natural fatigue resulting from the few hours of sleep. The only scare on the last day is when the fifth gear became inoperative, but this setback does not have any consequences since the technicians at Zuffenhausen, predicting the overworking of this component, have assembled the gearbox with almost the same ratios for fourth and fifth gear, thereby allowing for the use of either without affecting the top speed attained.

There is a huge collective sigh of relief when at 19:30 on the fourth day the record for the 20,000km is beaten with the fantastic average of 130mph (209.238km/h). Only half an hour is left to finish this memorable marathon and at 20:00 the 911 R turns into the pits, with its record-beating results registered by the FIA[22] delegate in attendance.

Despite the fatigue, the joy and the feeling of a job well done are everywhere. For me, besides the pleasure of living another unforgettable adventure from the inside, there is also the satisfaction of being a part of such an important event in the history of the marque!

The records attained at the Monza track were a remarkable feat for the time, reinforcing the marque's image and that of the 911, confirming its aptitude to become a winner in competitions. However, it was a completely unexpected feat for the 911, since the initial project was to use the 906. And it was in fact with a 906 that the attempt to beat the records started on 29 October. The instigators of this project were the Swiss Rico Steinemann and Dieter Spoerry, who put forward the idea using their own 906, with financial support from BP and Firestone and technical support from Porsche. It was then necessary to find two more drivers; Jo Siffert and Charles Vögele were available to join the project,

Before giving way to the 911 R, the 906 beat three international speed records (1,000 miles, 2,000km and six hours) at the Monza track.

leading to the creation of an entirely Swiss driving team. The choice of track fell on Monza, since its high-speed oval with a 38-degree incline offered the best option to get high speeds when compared to the other possibility of the French track of Linas–Montlhéry.

And so, at noon on 29 October, Jo Siffert and the 906 set off onto the track with a mission to beat several records held by Toyota and Ford. The first hours went well, with the 906 beating the records for the 1,000 miles, 2,000km and 6 hours. But the team had not taken into account the condition of the cement pavement of the speed oval at Monza, which, having been abandoned for a few years, was showing fissures and irregularities that meted out hard punishment upon the suspension. To make things harder, the FIA regulations forced all the likely parts for eventual repairs during the event to be transported inside the car. And so, even though the replacement of shock absorbers had been predicted, the three units on board the 906 were used during the first 12 hours of the race, leading to the car's early retirement from the record-breaking attempt when the fourth shock absorber gave out.

However, after the 906 stopped in the pits and then studying the regulations, the team realized that the record attempt could restart within 48 hours, even if using another car. An urgent phone call was made

been happier with this resounding result and first win at Daytona, in which the 'little' Porsches with their 2.2-litre engines have beaten the far more powerful Ford GT40s (with 5-litre engines) that were favoured to win.

The race passed without any major incidents for the team, except for the fourth 907 no.53 of Gerhard Mitter/Udo Schütz, which suffered a violent accident and retired from the race. Ford dominated the early race, but quickly the 907s climbed

The victorious 907 in the inner part of Daytona circuit.

The 907s pass the finish line, getting the first three places at the 1968 24 Hours of Daytona.

to the top places. In a race like this, one must take care in overtaking the slower cars of the group, since there is a huge difference in speed because tourism cars are admitted, like the Chevrolet Camaros and even Triumph Spitfires and Lancia Fulvias, among others.

Vic Elford always kept a lively pace, but also with enough care to avoid unpleasant surprises. Of course, the mechanical endurance of the cars is paramount in a 24-hour race, especially at a track as demanding as Daytona's, where a significant part of the distance is run at high speed on the 30-degree bank. The Porsche entrants once again proved their reliability. The victorious 907 ran 2,564 miles (4,126km) at an average of 106.83mph (171.9km/h).

This first victory in the 24 Hours of Daytona foreshadowed seventeen others that followed throughout the years (until 2003), opening up an era of Porsche domination in this famous American race. The 907 victorious at Daytona in a LH (Long Tail) version was an evolution of the models 906[24] and 910.[25]

In 1968, Porsche would go on to win three more races of the International Championship for Makes: with the 907, the 12 Hours of Sebring (Siffert/Elford) and the Targa Florio (Elford/Maglioli); with the 908, the 1,000km of the Nürburgring (Siffert/Elford). Porsche finished the championship in second place, preparing to attack the top title in the next year.

The frantic period that started in 1966 with the creation of the 906, followed by the 910, 907 and 908, was bearing fruit, showcasing the brand as the potential winner in any race circuit it entered. The private clients had quick access to buy these cars, which provided a significant financial input to allow for more research and development, but also the success in racing served as 'free' publicity and a motivation for the enormous number of fans that the brand was now amassing.

5 MAY 1968, CIRCUITO DELLE MADONIE, SICILY

Vic Elford opens the lock on the safety belt holding him in the seat of the 907 as quickly as possible and jumps out of the car that has just gone off the road on a slow corner. He realizes quickly that his right front tyre is flat, in addition to the problem that he had tried to repair when we stopped a few minutes before at the assistance point in Polizzi – the nut that holds the left rear wheel in place is loose again! After that, he opens the rear hood of the 907 and gets out the spare tyre and jack, replacing the flat tyre as fast as possible and tightening the nut of the rear wheel as best he can after that. He sits down in the car again, fastens the seat belt and darts off at full speed, fearing that his chance to win the Targa Florio has turned to smoke in the first lap of the race. Soon after, the vibrations of

The 907 of Vic Elford and Umberto Maglioli at the 1968 Targa Florio.

the rear axle return, a sign that the nut is loose yet again and he is forced to slow down, going down the straight at Campofelice at a speed well below normal.

The priority now is to be able to get to the main assistance point near Cerda, so that the mechanics can solve the problem; it is with great relief that when we get there, Elford turns the car slightly left to get on the road that provides access to the pit lane. The mechanics are finally able to get to the bottom of the problem and we set off again, with Vic Elford determined to recover as much time as possible. Almost 20 minutes were lost with the incidents of the first lap, which leaves us in a place well behind the first ten. But Elford, besides being an extraordinary driver, is also a fighter and gives it his all, performing the third lap of the Circuito Madonie in the spectacular time of 36min 02.3sec, establishing a new record and decreasing the disadvantage to the first cars by 5min 30sec!

Out in front the fight is between the Porsche 907 of Ludovico Scarfiotti and Gerhard Mitter in the lead, followed by the Alfa Romeo of Nino Vaccarella and Udo Schütz, then another works 907, driven by Hans Herrmann and Jochen Neerpasch. Vic Elford does another lap at a diabolical pace and we stop now at the end of the fourth lap to hand the 907 over to Umberto Maglioli, already in seventh position and 10 minutes behind the leader! Maglioli is an excellent connoisseur of the circuit and a former winner, but despite great driving he cannot match Elford's times, although he is fastest on the sixth lap.

The leader of the race is now the Alfa Romeo of Ignazio Giunti and Nanni Galli, as the 907 that was leading until then went off the road and is now back in sixth position. The Italians are now in a frenzy! We are on the seventh lap, Maglioli is still very fast and hands the car back to Elford for the last shift while in third position and little more than 2 minutes away from first place, which is still held

The 907 of Elford/Maglioli at the 1968 Targa Florio.

by Giunti/Galli's Alfa. Elford leaves the pit lane even more determined because he feels that victory is once again in his grasp. We are now in the most sinuous part of the circuit, with the turns following each other in rapid rhythm. The 907 glides from one to the other in a near magical way and Elford only wants to get close to the rear of the Alfa Romeo that is now his target!

During the ninth lap, to the desperation of the Italian fans, we quickly get close to the Alfa Romeo and overtake it. Elford smiles again, relieved, getting a lead of 1min 38sec at the start of the last lap. Elford does not slow his rhythm much and the advantage has been widened to 2min 43sec by the time we cross the line at the end of the tenth lap, victorious, to the delight of the entire team at a feat that seemed impossible after the initial 20-minute delay. It is a tired but extremely happy Elford who comes out of the 907 and hugs Maglioli, who is rejoicing at his third victory in the Targa Florio!

Without a doubt, this was one of the most beautiful wins for the 907 and Vic Elford, for whom 1968 was a very special year. After winning the Monte Carlo Rally in a 911 and, almost immediately after, the 24 Hours of Daytona in a 907, he won for the first time the very difficult Sicilian race due to his fantastic driving skills and a remarkable fighting spirit. His ability to win in diverse environments was thus confirmed, as well as making a vital contribution to Porsche's reputation for success in these charismatic racing events.

This victory at the Targa Florio was also the culmination of the 907's career in the service of Porsche, since the 908 took its place, continuing the success of a generation of cars that had started with the 906 in 1966. The 906, as well as its successors, the 910 and the 907, obtained countless victories in both circuits and hill-climb races (and even some rallies), whether through factory teams or in the hands of the many private drivers who bought them for use in the most diverse races. They were an excellent workhorse that lasted many years and to this day bring pleasure to the marque's fans when they make appearances at classic events in different locations.

26 SEPTEMBER 1969, BIARRITZ, FRANCE

After nine days of competition and 3,100 miles (5,000km) through the French roads (with an incursion into Germany and Belgium as well), we have arrived in Biarritz, where the Tour Auto ends. Thi is a very popular race in France, revamped this year after a four-year hiatus. The 911 R goes up to the podium, victorious at the hands of Gérard Larrousse and Maurice Gélin. It emits the traditional growling sound from its exhausts and displays a healthy look despite the harshness of the race. I had a lot of fun throughout this race, with its varied menu of road stages, racing circuits and even hill-climbing. It is a taxing race that demands rigorous technical and logistical preparation.

Now, at the moment of glory as the traditional colourful bands are placed over the hood of the 911 R, I recall some of the most significant moments lived in the last few days, such as: the climb of Mont Ventoux, where Larrousse, inspired, gained a 19 second lead over the second-place runner; the race on the legendary Nürburgring, with the spirited fight between Henri Greder in his powerful Corvette, who got his way at the end of the six laps, gaining 5 seconds over us; the twenty laps on the Spa-Francorchamps circuit; the race on the Reims circuit; the repetition of the battle with Greder on the Charade circuit, with great driving moments by Larrousse, who oversteered along some of the curves of the circuit

Gérard Larrousse drives the 911 R at a circuit stage of the 1969 Tour Auto.

Gerard Larrousse and Maurice Gélin win the 1969 Tour Auto in the 911 R after nine days of tough competition.

while Greder was jumping on the inside; and the final battle on the Nogaro circuit with Greder and Guy Chasseuil (Porsche 911).

These were, without a doubt, unforgettable days in this 911 R, which revealed itself once again to be an excellent competition machine, in all different types of races. And now, after the podium, the celebrations and champagne for the winners, comes the much deserved rest!

But later, all of a sudden in the parc fermé … surprise! … the engine of the 911 is heard again and, after revving up, we're rolling again. I think for a moment that the 911 R is being stolen, but then I recognize that it is Jürgen Barth[26] at the wheel, smiling and looking at the trophy resting on the passenger's seat. It is going to be a long night (but no doubt unforgettable!), as we pass through small French villages, then onto the national roads towards Zuffenhausen. Many French people next morning will wonder what that noise was that woke them in the middle of the night from their comforting slumber!

The car that had just won a race of 3,100 miles (5,000km), returned 'home' more than 620 miles (1,000km) away under its own steam, proving once again its endurance and versatility. Rico Steinemann (sport director), when he received the phone call in Stuttgart announcing the victory in the Tour Auto, immediately requested the chief mechanic, Jürgen Barth, to return quickly to deliver the trophy to Dr Ferry Porsche, who received it happily on Monday morning in his office in Zuffenhausen.

The 911 R that was victorious at the Tour Auto was the no.5 chassis. It was one of those reserved by the factory for its own use and became the most well-known, after another victory later in the year at the Tour de Corse rally (also with Larrousse and Gélin).

THE GOLDEN ERA: THE 1970s AND 1980s

24 JANUARY 1970, MONTE CARLO, PRINCIPALITY OF MONACO

It's almost 04:30 and before me I see zigzagging trees and snow banks that line the road passing by, illuminated by powerful additional headlights installed on top of the hood of the orange 911 S no.2, driven by Gérard Larrousse. The night is dark and cold, but the atmosphere inside the car is warm and almost 'frantic', thanks to the hoarse sound of the flat-6. Maurice Gélin 'sings' the pace notes to Larrousse, clearly and confidently. We are in the most charismatic special stage of the Monte Carlo Rally, the one that takes competitors from La Bollène-Vésubie to Moulinet, and whose high point is the passage through the famous Col de Turini. We are now a few hundred yards from this spot, where, in accordance with tradition there are many spectators, indifferent to time and cold, to cheer on their idols. Gélin has just dictated: '50 metres, droite 60, Attention! Verglas! 40 metres, 50 gauche.'[27] When we enter the announced right corner, the night becomes almost day, due to the flashes of the cameras, which are reflected in the snow, on the road and off the side banks. It is the madness of the spectators, who always expect a special show from the drivers in these brief seconds that we are in front of them, before plunging into the descent, which follows the next curve to the left, leading us to the village of Moulinet.

Larrousse strives to the maximum, because we are in an open fight with Jean-Pierre Nicolas (Alpine-Renault) for second position in the overall standings, as in the lead is our very confident teammate Björn Waldegård in the 911 no.6. Bjorn has dominated the rally from the beginning and now, two special stages from the end (including the one on which we are) he has a lead of 2 minutes, allowing him to control the race. But the fight for second place is fierce and is going on from the beginning of this final leg of the rally, when we left Monte Carlo in third position 2 seconds behind Nicolas. It is a fight not only about driving and a test of nerves, but also about the judgments that need to made about what tyres to use, for example. And in a 'Monte' where there is little snow, as this year, the choices are even more difficult, because in the same stage there are completely dry areas, but others with snow or even ice.

The 911 S of Gérard Larrousse and Maurice Gélin finished in second place the 1970 Monte Carlo rally behind the sister car of teammates Björn Waldegård and Lars Helmer.

The big question is between the choice of studded tyres (how many and what size?) and normal tyres, with the first ones being an insurance against snow and ice, but wasting too much time on dry asphalt. The choice is always based on a cost-benefit analysis, but it is very easy to fail, because the conditions found on the road can change quickly. And for this special stage, the situation is indeed complicated, because for the 14 miles (23km) of its total length, 4.4 miles (7km) of those present snow and ice, with the aggravating circumstance of needing to be travelled three times during this leg. Everybody knows that it's often this stage that decides the rally.

And this time it is no different, as on the first pass Nicolas gained 54 seconds over us due to our wrong choice of tyres (with long studs), which caused difficulties for us in the dry conditions and led to three spins. In the overall standings we were at that time in third position, 1min 9sec behind Nicolas. For the next passage we correct the tyre choice, and combined with the committed and inspired driving of Larrousse, we have a 1 second lead over Nicolas. Hence the commitment of Larrousse in this last passage, in which everything will be decided. We continue to attack on this dangerous descent, the powerful headlights cutting through the darkness and showing the way through the well-known Alpine roads with stone walls on one side and cliffs on the other.

The 7.45 miles (12km) descent is done at a breakneck pace. We are now coming to the checkpoint, Larrousse brakes firmly at the last moment, causing the brakes to squeal. Gélin opens the window and gives the timing card to the controller, who records a time of 21min 51sec. So we have gained more than 10 seconds over Nicolas and as we had also won the previous stage, we are now 47 seconds ahead, before the final stage, Peille.

In this last stage, Larrousse lifts his right foot a bit, ensuring the position, but we still gain another 4 seconds. Tired but happy, Larrousse and Gélin greet each other, having achieved their goal. Now they just have to take the car to Albert I pier, in Monte Carlo Bay. When we arrive, a little after 06:00, the cars of Waldegård/Helmer and Nicolas/Roure are already there and soon after the other car of the Porsche team arrives, the Anderson/Thorszelius 911 no.11, which finished fourth and sealed the overall performance of the marque. For me it was an unforgettable week, since the start in Warsaw eight days ago, until the arrival at the Principality on the last day. Thanks to Gérard Larrousse and Maurice Gélin!

This was the second consecutive victory in the most famous rally in the world for Björn Waldegård and Lars Helmer and the third in a row for Porsche, who had achieved its first victory there in 1968, with Vic Elford and David Stone.

The 911 was confirmed as a great rally car that could fight for victory in any event of the World Championship, but winning at Monte Carlo was always very special because of its enormous prestige. Its format was also unique and very demanding because there was a total of about 3,400 miles (5,500km) to be covered over eight days. There was the Concentration Section first, departing from eight European cities, from which competitors could choose freely. In 1970, the cities with most teams departing, in addition to Monte Carlo with forty-three, were Reims with twenty-eight and Oslo with twenty-seven. There were also departures from Frankfurt, Dover, Lisbon, Warsaw and Athens; the total number of competitors was 184. All the different itineraries had a similar distance of around 2,113 miles (3,400km), where there were no special stages and the drivers were 'only' required to fulfil an average speed of 37.2mph (60km/h). This was to give an international image to the event and to start to fatigue the teams before the actual start of hostilities in the Common Section, with 947 miles (1,524km), on a route beginning and ending in the Principality, with nine special stages.

The last leg was exclusively reserved for the first sixty classified at the end of the previous journey. It was during the night that everything was decided, with the toughest stages, including three passes through the Col de Turini. To claim victory, it was no longer enough to be a good driver with a good car, because those not belonging to a factory team would stand no chance. The officially enrolled teams that year were Porsche (three cars), Alpine-Renault (four cars), Lancia (six cars), Ford (four cars) and Toyota (two cars). Porsche, besides its superiority in performance, impressed with its reliability because all its cars managed to finish the rally.

The cars used were 911 S, with a 2247cc/240bhp engine and a weight of 1,852lb (840kg). They were by far the most powerful cars, but the achievement of victory, in addition to the skill of the drivers, was also due to careful preparation and an impeccably organized technical assistance team.

20–21 MARCH 1970, SEBRING, USA

The Sebring track, which uses parts of an airfield, has been known to the drivers and brands in the World Sportscar Championship for some years. The 12-hour race is the second of the Championship, practice is under way and the car in which I now find myself is quite different from the one in my last adventures (the 911 of Larrousse/Gélin in the Monte Carlo Rally) since my new 'address' is now a 908 that is going to be driven by Steve McQueen and Peter Revson. Larrousse is also attending Sebring in another 908, but having heard about Steve McQueen's charismatic figure, I decided to 'switch' 908s, to have the opportunity of getting to know this famous actor-driver, as well as his partner, the skilled American driver, Peter Revson.

Moving from road races to circuits, there is also the possibility of accompanying endurance races this season, which look promising for Porsche and in which the 917 will certainly play an important part. But here at Sebring there is a white 908 no.48 to enjoy, gorgeous and almost advertising-free. It is the Flunder model, which is the last evolution of the body for this model, more aerodynamic, thanks to its purer lines, than the original model.

Steve McQueen in the 908/2 'Flunder' laps a GT Corvette at the 1970 12 Hours of Sebring.

Steve McQueen is somewhat debilitated, having broken a foot recently (in a motorcycle race accident) and still being in a plaster cast, for which it has been necessary to build a special cover. But that has not shaken his good mood and his will to give it his all, with the team getting the fifteenth best time in practice, being the fastest 908 attending, although almost 8 seconds away from the best 917. The fastest lap was done by the Ferrari 512 of Mario Andretti/Arturo Merzario.

The 12-hour race has developed into a battle between the Porsche 917s and the Ferrari 512s, alternating in which leads the race. At the end of the third hour, the race is led by a set of three Ferraris and it seems they could make life quite difficult for the Stuttgart brand. But, as the hours advance, many retire from the race and our 908 starts climbing in the standings.

Halfway through the race, the three Ferraris are still ahead and our 908/2 is right after them. The 917s have had several problems – John Wyer's car with problems in the hubs and engine and Vic Elford's car due to a crash. But, after that, the Ferraris have run into problems, letting us move up into second place behind the Ferrari of Andretti/Merzario.

And then the unexpected happens. With 1 hour to go, the Ferrari is forced to abandon the race and the new race leaders become … McQueen and Revson! The team rejoices, but nothing is guaranteed, because behind us the 917 of Pedro Rodriguez and Leo Kinnunen and the 512 of Ignazio Giunti and Nino Vaccarella are recovering ground quickly. It is an open-ended race, but it is impossible for the 908 to stand up to the power difference of the Sport class cars. Ferrari goes all out and puts Mario Andretti in Giunti/Vacarella's car, trying to fight the superior speed of the Rodriguez/Kinnunen team, which soon climbs to first place, followed by the Ferrari.

Steve McQueen's 908 in front of the Siffert/Redman 917 at the 1970 12 Hours of Sebring.

And all of a sudden, more drama, as the 917 that is in the lead is forced to make a pit stop that lasts 8 minutes, with Andretti's 512 taking the lead. Just 5 minutes from the end our second place is looking excellent, but once again there is suspense, since the Ferrari has to make a quick stop in the pits to take in some fuel, which allows us to make a final push. Andretti sets off desperately, giving it his best and he is able to cross the finish line with a scarce 20-second lead over our 908!

Without a doubt a fantastic race and unexpected for us, winning Porsche important points for the Championship and compensating for a not so good race by the 917s. And for me it was a pleasure to be driven by Peter Revson and Steve McQueen!

This second race for the 1970 Championship was an interesting one and it is curious that a few years later, there was a theory, put forward by one of the race marshals, stating that McQueen/Revson's 908 could have actually won the race, since there was an error in counting the completed laps and one lap fewer had been counted from those actually completed. One must take into account that in 1970 there was no electronic system for timing or lap counting and that the times and laps were registered by a battalion of race marshals, who were responsible for this hard task, especially for the laps done during the night. Thus, there will always be this small doubt of an eventual victory of the 908/2 no.48 in the 12 Hours of Sebring in 1970!

12 APRIL 1970, BRANDS HATCH, UK

It is raining non-stop and water skates across the sloping track where the Brands Hatch 1,000km will be held for the World Sportcars Championship. At last, the 917...! It is chassis no.016, with drivers Pedro Rodriguez and Leo Kinnunen. In the middle of the third row of the starting grid, we're getting ready for the off. Rodriguez, after his win at Daytona and fourth place at Sebring, is keen to return to first place on the podium, so will surely start flat out.

In front of us, on the first row, are the two Ferrari 512s of Chris Amon/Arturo Merzario and Jacky Ickx/Jackie Oliver, with the 917 of Vic Elford/Dennis Hulme. On the second row are the Matra 650 of Jack Brabham/Jean-Pierre Beltoise and the other John Wyer Porsche 917 of Jo Siffert/Brian Redman. On the third row we occupy the central position alongside the Matra 650 of Henri Pescarolo/Johnny Servoz-Gavin, with the Alfa Romeo 33 of Piers Courage/Andrea de Adamich next to us.

At 12:00 on the dot, the race is started and the fight for first position starts immediately, despite the unfavourable conditions. Jacky Ickx reacts first and sets out in the lead, but Vic Elford attacks at the first turn, Paddock Bend, and takes the lead. In the middle of the pack the alarm sounds, because due to the large amount of water on the track, a Lola goes into an aquaplaning skid, hits the barrier and comes back to the track, leaving a trail of wreckage. Yellow flags are shown and with the first lap coming to an end Elford (917) is in command, followed by Ickx (Ferrari 512), with us having moved into the sixth position.

But on one of the next passes across the start/finish line we are shown the black flag, which means we have to go into the pit lane at the end of the lap and stop. An unhappy Rodriguez does so and is informed by the race director,

Ferrari and Porsche fight for the lead after the start of the Brands Hatch 1,000km.

Pedro Rodriguez drove the 917 for five and a half hours, performing an extraordinary and unforgettable 'recital' to the spectators at the Brands Hatch 1,000km.

that this penalty is due to the fact that we overtook another driver while under the yellow flag. He sets off again at full power, sliding on the wet ground, even more determined to take the no.10 917 into the top positions.

The next several laps are pure magic. Rodriguez, the master of rain, plays his concerto: we quickly pass Brabham (Matra) and Amon (Ferrari) and on the tenth lap, at the exit of Clearways corner, he attacks Elford. We go through the start/finish straight side by side, the crowd standing and cheering. As we arrive at Paddock Bend, Rodriguez dives the 917 into the inside of the turn and we exit in front. Rodriguez is on a roll and we gain 5 seconds per lap over our direct competitors. They are adrenalin-filled moments, the purest symbiosis between man and machine that I will ever forget! The lead over all the other runners is increasing rapidly and Rodriguez is so excited and committed to his work that he does not relinquish his place to Kinnunen when he stops to refuel, continuing at a hellish pace and soon getting a complete lap's advantage over Elford.

After 3 hours of racing and 264.7 miles (426km) completed under such adverse conditions, our advantage is already two laps over the 917 of Siffert/Redman, three laps over the 917 of Elford/Hulme and six laps over the Ferrari of Amon/ Merzario. Only when 3.5 hours have passed and the rain stops, does Rodriguez hand over the wheel to the young Kinnunen. The Finnish man manages to hold the pressure and loses little time to his pursuers, but Rodriguez is eager to get back in the action and after 1.25 hours he's already at the wheel again for the final push. His driving is so outstanding that with 200 laps completed, his lead over the second runner (now the 917 of Elford/Hulme) is currently five laps! This lead is maintained for the remaining thirty-five laps and Rodriguez crosses the finish line victorious at the end of 1,000km, after a show of great bravery and a superior class of driving. The crowd can feel that they watched, without a doubt, a great exhibition by a great driver, who astonished everyone for 5.5 hours of the 6hr 45min that the race lasted. Simply brilliant!

The 917 of Rodriguez/ Kinnunen finished its victorious race with a five-lap lead over the 917 of Elford/ Hulme.

Porsche, with this dominating victory, in which it got the four top places in the overall standing, consolidated its lead in the Championship and showed that it would have hardly any competitive adversaries in the remaining seven races. The Championship, however, would not lose its interest because the fight for wins between the John Wyer and the Porsche KG Salzburg teams would generate moments of rivalry and uncertainty as to the winners of each race.

Pedro Rodriguez (with cap and sunglasses) behind the 917 at Brands Hatch circuit.

3 MAY 1970, CIRCUITO DELLE MADONIE, SICILY

The four 'aces' that came from Stuttgart are on display in the middle of a stone-made roundabout and they are presented for the first time to reporters. I'm referring to four 908/3s, a completely new variant of the 908 that was conceived specially to race in the Targa Florio. It's a small car, light (1,214lb/550kg), powerful (380bhp) and extremely agile, ideal to run the race on the sinuous track of the 'Madonies' that goes along public roads for 44.75 miles (72km) and with over 800 curves.

The four 'aces' in Sicily ready to race in the 1970 Targa Florio. From left: Jo Siffet, John Wyer, Ferdinand Piech and Vic Elford.

Porsche, in deciding to make a specific car for this race (but also in the hope of increasing its chances at Nürburgring) shows promptly what its level of commitment to win the Championship is, since it is clear that the 917s are too big and powerful for this type of circuit.

But why four aces? Designer Tony Lapine decided to give a bit of colour and originality to the decoration of the cars sent to the Sicilian race.[28] Thus we have: the 'ace of diamonds', with no.12, for the Jo Siffert/Brian Redman team, painted in the traditional Gulf Blue and with two large orange arrows on each side of the cockpit, along the entire length of the car; the 'ace of clubs', with no.36 (Richard Attwood/Björn Waldegård), also in the 'Gulf' colours, but with a single arrow painted at full width on the front of the car; the 'ace of spades', with no.40 (Pedro Rodriguez/Leo Kinnunen), yet another with the Gulf colours, with a single arrow on the left side of the cockpit; and the 'ace of hearts', with no.20 (Vic Elford/Hans Herrmann), painted in white, with several transversal curved stripes, painted in red. The first three are enrolled by John Wyer and the last one by Porsche KG Salzburg.

The official practice will only happen on Thursday, but incredible as it may seem, all the brands will continue to do their tests on Friday and Saturday with the roads … open to normal traffic!! It's scary, but I'm prepared to live this incredible adventure again and this time my money is on the 'ace of diamonds' (chassis no.008) – 'Messieurs [les pilotes] faites vos jeux!'.[29]

It's impressive to go through these narrow roads (almost) at race pace, whizzing through villages, with cars, people and animals next to the houses … as long as they don't decide to cross to the other side of the road! We're going through the village of Cerda, Siffert pays close attention, since he knows that at

Jo Siffert drives the 908/3 amidst the unique Targa Florio race scenery.

*any time some 'surprise' might pop up, coming from a narrow crossing, or from
a doorway. We're going at almost 124mph (200km/h) among houses, with the
kerbs of the narrow footpaths on the sides of the asphalt. It's breathtaking, but in
fact everything is under control and we're already going towards Sclafani Bagni.*

*The driving pace, imposed by the shape of the terrain, is infernal, testing the
ability of the driver, but also the agility of the car and its mechanical endurance.
The 908/3 takes everything in its stride and the miles pass at an impressive rate.
We're now going up towards Caltavuturo, with its famous crossing indicating in
opposite directions Palermo and Campofelice, where we are headed now. The
road goes downhill a bit until Collesano, then descends more steeply until sea
level at Campofelice. After this village starts the longest straight of the circuit,
Buonfornello, at 3.7 miles (6km), and this is practically the only area of the circuit
where the more powerful cars have an advantage over the more agile ones. It is
on this straight that we can get to the top speed of the 908/3, which is 172mph
(277km/h).*

*With the long straight finished, we are back on a sinuous road that takes us
to the start/finish line. In the official practice on Thursday, Siffert manages the
best time, with 34min 10sec to complete the 45 miles (72km) of the circuit, at an
average above 78.3mph (126km/h), beating the old record by almost a minute,
thus proving the power of the 908/3. In the following positions are: Vic Elford in
the 908/3 'ace of hearts'; Nino Vaccarella, the Italian driver born in Palermo, idol
of the Sicilians, in a Ferrari 512 S (but 36 seconds behind Siffert); Piers Courage
and Andrea de Adamich, both in Alfa Romeo 33s.*

*On the day of the race, which starts off rainy, 400,000 spectators are lining
the circuit longing for the victory of their idol. The start has to be postponed for
1 hour, due to the weather and track conditions, since there is mud in some areas.
The proceedings for the start are quite peculiar here, since it is impossible to form
a starting grid with the cars because of the narrowness of the road, so each driver
is sent off individually, at 15-second intervals. When the race director shows us
the start flag, Siffert sets off confidently, but with caution, due to the unfavourable conditions. Some of the drivers are going to be surprised in this first lap, one
of them being Elford, who crashes after having driven only 9 miles (15km). The
time done by us in the first lap (40min 35sec) shows well the difficulties we have
encountered and it is Gérard Larrousse (as the experienced rallyman that he is)
who is in the lead in a 908/2, having completed the circuit in 13 seconds fewer
than us. On the second lap, Siffert manages to reduce the difference to 7 seconds
and right after us is Rodriguez in the 'ace of spades'.*

*The Mexican is now flat out and is leading at the end of the third lap. Siffert,
due to a lack of information about our standing, has let the pace drop and we
are now in sixth position. On the fourth lap, there is a pit stop for refuelling and
Redman takes the wheel in the 'ace of diamonds', but Kinnunen, who replaced
Rodriguez, is able to maintain his lead.*

During a pit stop, Brian Redman has just handed over the 908/3 to Jo Siffert.

Jo Siffert and Brian Redman in the 908/3 gave Porsche its tenth victory at the Targa Florio.

The weather conditions improve and Vaccarella is the one who is now driving a brilliant race, since he is the most knowledgeable about this circuit. He is able to overcome the difficulties of driving the large 512 and manages to overtake us, taking over second position. On the sixth lap, Vaccarella takes the lead and the Sicilian crowd goes wild, but his advantage is only 1 second over the second runner, which is … our 'ace of diamonds'! Redman is on the offensive, and at the end of the seventh lap we take the lead with 3.7sec over Vaccarella's Ferrari, which starts to experience steering problems. His dream, and that of his country-men, soon disappears and by the eighth lap the lead of the 'ace of diamonds' is already 14 seconds.

Kinnunen, who replaced Rodriguez in the 'ace of spades', is now driving a spec-tacular race, and he even passes the Ferrari 512 (driven now by Giunti), which, due to the 'appetite' of its V12 engine, has to make a supplementary stop to refuel. Vaccarella retakes the wheel and darts off, gritting his teeth, as he knows that a second place finish is still possible. With the tenth (and second to last) lap completed, he is able to retake the second position with 10.9sec over Kinnunen, but the Finnish man is in a state of grace today and does a fantastic last lap in 33min 36sec, destroying the lap record, and gaining 2 minutes over Vaccarella, who has to be content with third position.

But the victory festivities in the end are for our 'ace of diamonds', which, after the eleven laps, almost 9,000 turns and 6hr 35min, goes through the finish line in first place, fulfilling the objectives for which it was created and making Siffert and Redman, who win for the first time on the very hard Sicilian circuit, extremely happy men. As for me, even though it is a repetition, the pleasure is the same, and in fact it is impressive to attest to the extraordinary qualities of this small marvel that is the 908/3, which has revealed itself to be a true ace on the sinu-ous roads of Sicily.

It is interesting to note that this victory by Siffert/Redman almost did not happen, since during the last lap a quick stop was planned at Polizzi, halfway through the circuit, to take on a few more litres of fuel, but Siffert missed the stop at the correct location. He therefore had to take the rest of the lap saving fuel, and 'praying' that the warning light, that came on immediately, was not the announcement of another 'almost' win in the Targa Florio.

The 908/3 also shone as a team, since besides the two first positions of Siffert/Herrmann and Rodriguez/Kinnunen, the 'ace of clubs' of Attwood/Waldegård got fifth position, behind the Ferrari of Giunti/Vaccarella and the 908/2 of Laine/Van Lennep. In the 1970 World Championship, the 908/3 would prove again its value by winning at the difficult Nürbur-gring circuit in the 1,000km race, with the winning drivers being Elford/Ahrens, in front of another 908/3 with Herrmann/Attwood.

17 MAY 1970, SPA-FRANCORCHAMPS, BELGIUM

Two weeks have passed after the strong emotions of the Targa Florio, the slowest circuit of the Championship, and we are now at the fastest track of all – Spa, where the average speed exceeds 149mph (240km/h). This circuit has several breathtaking points, but Eau Rouge, at the end of the descent that starts from La Source corner and culminates in the left curve of Raidillon, surpasses all the others. Here only drivers with well above-average skills can demand from their cars all they have to offer! It takes a good dose of virtuosity, courage and confidence to negotiate this part of the track without using the brake pedal.

This year, the expectation of what the Porsche 917s and Ferrari 512s will perform in this ultra-fast circuit feeds many lively conversations, betting among enthusiasts and questions among the drivers. So far, the fastest lap done here was the work of the great champion Jim Clark, who in 1967, in the Belgian Formula One Grand Prix, achieved the time of 3min 28sec with an average speed of 151.6mph (244km/h). Will the current sport cars exceed this mark and beat the Formula Ones?

I am very anxious to be able to witness these events in the most direct way possible, so I just had to keep my 'connection' to the Siffert/Redman team to secure a place in the first row! The 917 with chassis no.004 will be the weapon to use and I am sure will do the job very well.

The first day of practice went by with variable weather conditions, but one could see the potential of the fastest cars on the track: the Belgian Jacky Ickx, racing at home with the Ferrari 512, quickly broke Jim Clark's record when he completed a lap in 3min 24sec, thereby removing 4 seconds from the Lotus 49's time. Pedro Rodriguez in the other John Wyer 917 did 3min 27sec. As for our 917, it gave us a great shock, because when we were driving at more than 205mph (330km/h) on the descent towards Stavelot, the left front tyre decided to abandon us and it was only thanks to Siffert's expertise and some luck that the 917 stopped without major damage.

On the second day of practice with a completely dry track, the previous times were pulverized: Pedro Rodriguez got the fabulous time of 3min 18.8sec at the extraordinary average speed of 157.8mph (254km/h)! Siffert did his best lap in 3min 23.9sec, maybe a little affected by the tyre incident of the previous day, but still managed a second place on the grid, ahead of the Ickx/Surtees Ferrari 512.

The race thus promises a gripping Porsche–Ferrari duel, but also within the John Wyer team, where the rivalry between the two sets of drivers is well known. On race day it rained heavily during the morning, flooding the track, but 15 minutes before departure the rain stopped, to be replaced by a warm sun. The track will certainly take three or four laps to dry and the teams are struggling now with the difficulty of choosing tyres. The two 917s of our team will begin the race with intermediate tyres, as will the Ferrari of Jacky Ickx.

We are now close to 13:00 and the tension grows among all the actors in this challenging race. After the traditional recognition lap, our 917 no.24 stops before the start/finish line at the side of the 'sister' car, no.25. Siffert and Rodriguez look at each other briefly and then focus their attention on the starter, and at the same time at a point down at the end of the descent, the apex of the left curve of Eau Rouge, where it will be essential to enter with a perfect trajectory to ensure the command at the top of the Raidillon. The race director waits for everybody to stop on the grid, the expectation increases and finally the flag is lowered, freeing the thirty-five powerful and noisy cars. Jo Siffert accelerates decidedly, up to the limit tolerated by the wet track and the 917 starts raising a spray of water with its wide rear tyres at the grip limit, but Rodriguez is doing exactly the same and the two cars are side by side, without either gaining advantage.

The first corner of Eau Rouge is approaching fast and it seems that neither is willing to compromise. Rodriguez, who is on the left side of the track, is better positioned for its approach, but Siffert does not give up. Neither one brakes; I feel the cars touching, scraping the sides. Siffert touches lightly on the brake pedal and we are already in the right turn at the beginning of the climb to the Raidillon. The two cars are still side by side, but now the advantage is ours, because we are on the inner side of the curve and we finally manage to gain the advantage and get ahead in the difficult left turn at the top of the climb.

The epic fight between Jo Siffert and Pedro Rodriguez at the start of the 1970 Spa 1,000km will remain as one of the most remarkable in motorsport history.

RIGHT: **Jo Siffert (no.24) and Pedro Rodriguez (no.25) were the protagonists of a fantastic duel at the Spa-Francorchamps circuit under very difficult track conditions.**

BELOW: **The Porsche 917 of Siffert/Redman conquered at the 1970 Spa 1,000km, one of the most famous Porsche 917 victories in endurance racing.**

These are moments of high tension for those in the cockpits and without a doubt one of the most extraordinary of motor racing, much to the delight of the spectators who are being treated to a duel of giants! The fight for first place lasts for almost the whole race, not only between the two 917s alternating in the position, but also with the entry into the fray of the Ferrari 512 of Ickx/Surtees.

The doubt about the winner increases as the lap record is successively beaten and also according to the pit stops for refuelling. The times obtained clearly show the intensity of the struggle for victory and the capabilities demonstrated by both cars and drivers. Siffert and Rodriguez run systematically below 3min 23sec and when the duel reaches its peak Rodriguez does 3min 21.6sec. Siffert responds with 3min 20sec, followed by 3min 17.8sec, but then Rodriguez, who is trying to make up for lost time with an unscheduled pit stop, gets a whopping

3min 16.5sec mark that will remain as the lap record at an incredible average of 160.53mph (258.3km/h).

At this pace, the 1,000km race is quickly coming to an end, despite the struggle for victory having slowed down a bit after the withdrawal of Rodriguez/Kinnunen with gearbox problems. The chequered flag is lowered after 4hr 9min, with the victory going to our 917 no.24, beating the Ferrari team (Ickx/Surtees) by 2min 3sec.

It has indeed been a memorable race for drivers and spectators, and I dare to say I enjoyed it from the most spectacular observation point of all!

13–14 JUNE 1970, CIRCUIT DE LA SARTHE, LE MANS, FRANCE

16:00

Lined up at the start/finish straight at the legendary French circuit, I feel once again all the emotion that comes with preparing for the start of this most prestigious and famous race. In this edition of the 24 Hours of Le Mans, fifty-one cars are lined up diagonally, next to the pit wall, and it is the first time that the race will be started without the traditional driver sprint, crossing the track to take their seats. For safety reasons this procedure has been abandoned, but the expectation and emotion aren't any the less because of it.

I have the privilege of 'living' these 24 hours in the no.23 car, which will be driven by Hans Herrmann, with whom I've had the opportunity to live through fantastic moments already, and Richard Attwood, a calm and phlegmatic Englishman. I hesitated when I thought up my strategy to 'migrate' to one of the fabulous machines that Porsche brought to Le Mans, a grand total of twenty-seven cars among the fifty-one contenders.

The choice was difficult since it will surely be the first year in which the brand has the possibility of reaching an overall win (even though it almost achieved it in the previous year). With this objective, there are eight Porsche 917s, split into two factory teams, John Wyer and the Austrian branch, Porsche KG Salzburg, and two independent teams, Martini Racing and the one belonging to the English driver David Piper. To make the choice even harder, one has to consider that not all the cars are identical. On the body level there are two versions, the Short and the Long Tail (to make the most of the Hunaudières Straight), and as to the engines there are also two possibilities, the 4.5-litre, older and more reliable, and the newest 4.9-litre, which is surely more powerful but not as thoroughly tested. I confess that my first choice would be a Long Tail, but due to a variety of circumstances, I ended up finding a place on the no.23 chassis (curiously matching the number for the race).

Hans Herrmann and Richard Attwood, maybe due to the car that they are driving, a 917 K ('Kurz', short-tail) with a 4.5-litre engine, seem set on a more

After the 1970 24 Hours of Le Mans start, Porsche 917 no.23 of Hans Herrmann and Richard Attwood is in the middle of the pack with the 908 of Helmut Marko and Rudi Lins at its side.

conservative tactic, since we're on the fourteenth position of the starting grid, with the time of 3min 31.5sec, well behind the pole-position of Vic Elford in the 917LH ('Langheck', long-tail) no.25 with 3min 19.8sec. Thus we are positioned between a Ferrari 512 and a Matra 650, but this does not seem to bother Attwood, who is quite calm at the wheel, well aware that in a 24-hour race a lot can happen. His gaze is now set on the person that will signal the start and in this running of the race it is none other than Ferry Porsche, to whom the ACO (Automobile Club de l'Ouest) wants to pay homage for his twentieth participation in the race, a run that started brilliantly in 1951 with the 356 SL coupés. Will this be a good omen for Porsche's aspirations?

At 16:00 on the dot, Ferry Porsche waves the French flag and Attwood's left hand jumps quickly from the fuel-pump switch to the drilled starter key. The powerful growl of the flat-12 fills the cockpit, the 917 jumps on to the track, in the middle of a pack of cars whose thousands of horsepower cause a near supernatural sound, echoing between the track and the stands, which are crowded with thousands of spectators.

The 917LH of Vic Elford is already out in front, taking behind it the mob of fifty cars involved in this great adventure. Richard Attwood is determined not to take unnecessary risks, while also defending his position. The first lap goes by without incident and at the first pass across the line the red Porsche with white stripes, no.23, comes in twelfth position between the red 512S Ferrari of Jacky Ickx and the identical but yellow car of Jo Bonnier. Out in front the fight is rough between the Porsches and Ferraris, with the Matras and Lolas right behind them in waiting.

As a young man of fifteen years old, I'm 1,000 miles (1,600km) away from Le Mans, 'glued' to the television, watching the start of the 1970 24 Hours of Le Mans through the Eurovision broadcast. At this time, still with black and white images, we can only watch the last preparations before the start and the first half hour of the race, and then on Sunday a brief summary at the end of the morning and the last half hour of racing.

I was already completely obsessed with motor sports, especially with the Sport-prototype races and GTs that were part of the World Sportscar Championship, but I was specially fascinated by the 24-hour race at the de la Sarthe circuit, since the first time I had seen it, the previous year, the Porsche 908 of Herrmann/Larrousse had fought for the victory until the last few metres with the Ford GT40 of Ickx/Redman. My fascination for the Stuttgart brand had awakened over the last couple of years, with the discovery of the fantastic lines of a 911 that had passed by me and had made my head turn, fascinated by its shapes and unmistakable sound. I followed it, almost hypnotized, until it disappeared in the distance, like an inspiring mirage in a desert of boredom! The 'click' had happened and when I discovered that the 911 was a major player in international rallies and endurance races, this passion could only grow. I wanted to follow everything that the marque did, whether it was about the cars being sold to the public, or its involvement in automotive sport.

It is because of that, with great expectations, I am paying even more attention to the race this year, since Porsche has a real chance of winning. On the television I watch the cars line up next to the pit wall. We're almost at 16:00 and the commentator explains the new start procedures, lamenting the removal of the initial drivers' race across the track towards their cars. On the small screen there is now one of the favourites of the French enthusiasts, the Matra 650 of Jack Brabham and François Cévert, showing us Brabham calmly fastening his seat belt. Then all of a sudden comes the 'boom' of cars starting off! The director is caught completely off guard and when the cameras switch to the perspective of the start/finish straight, the leaders are already at the Dunlop turn. I follow with great emotion that first lap, watching the 917s of Vic Elford and Jo Siffert fighting for the lead, in a risky but beautiful 'ballet'. Once again, the 'mystique' of the binomial cars/circuit is confirmed, repeating itself every year in June, to the excitement of many thousands of fans who crowd the circuit, coming not only from France but also from many countries in Europe. It is a unique and awe-inspiring spectacle. While it may be dangerous for those directly involved in the race, a win in the 24 Hours of Le Mans is so prestigious that it will bring great rewards to the winning marque, more so than victory in the Championship in which it is included.

The half-hour broadcast quickly comes to an end. The Porsche cars are out in front, but the Ferraris are a threat. The expectation as to Porsche's performance is enormous and it is nerve-racking to have to wait for the news broadcast on Sunday. Until then, how can one get news about the race developments? Will the Stuttgart cars survive the pressure?

17:00

Passing at Arnage we see Pedro Rodriguez and Leo Kinnunen's 917 stopped on the side, which they will abandon shortly with engine problems. A light drizzle starts to fall…

17:45

Pit stop and driver change. In comes Hans Herrmann, my 'old acquaintance' from other battles. It is remarkable that he raced for the first time here in Le Mans in 1953 and is still driving at his best level. He is without a doubt an 'old fox', and it is always a pleasure to be driven by a master with such an impressive résumé.

18:28

We pass three Ferrari 512s, which were involved in a chain-reaction crash in the Maison Blanche area and they are forced to retire. Shortly after, another 512 withdraws from the race when its engine 'explodes' right in the Hunaudières Straight, with Derek Bell at the wheel. We haven't completed 3 hours of racing and the list of retired cars amongst those who had a claim at winning is already notable! The rain intensifies, making the driving even more difficult and demanding.

Hour after hour, the 917 of Hans Herrmann and Richard Attwood overtakes its opponents and approaches the top of the classification.

19:05

In the lead are still the 917s of Vic Elford/Kurt Ahrens and Jo Siffert/Brian Redman, but we continue to move up in the standings and are now in sixth place. Certainly, some of it is due to the misfortune of others, but it is also due to the tactics adopted by the team and in a marathon such as this, only at the end is it known who made the best bet.

19:33

A veritable storm falls on the circuit and we cannot drive under 5 minutes per lap. One cannot be careful enough to keep the car on the track and avoid 'traps' and other less cautious drivers.

20:00

The rain becomes less intense. We go up two more spots in the standings and the car is still working perfectly.

22:07

We go down into sixth position, not because we have experienced any problems, but because the 917 of Gérard Larrousse/Willi Kauhsen and the Ferrari 512 of Jacky Ickx/Peter Schetty have recovered the time they had previously lost. We pass the no.18 917 of Gijs van Lennep/David Piper, which was ahead of us in the standings, but has crashed at the Dunlop turn.

00:00

Eight hours of racing and we're up to third position, since the no.25 917 with Elford at the wheel has had to stop twice due to flat tyres and lost over 8 minutes. Siffert is in the lead and Ickx is second, but four laps away, with us one lap behind the Ferrari.

01:35

Drama at the circuit. At the Ford Chicane, Ickx's Ferrari, after an unbalanced braking, spins, then goes into the dirt barrier, which slings it over the fence. It hits a race marshall, who eventually dies. The world of motor racing is certainly not without its tragedies.

02:00

At the beginning of the tenth hour of the race we are in second position, seven laps away from the 917 of Siffert/Redman. The headlights sweep the night and guide us through the turns and the GT category cars, which become moving 'chicanes', because the difference in speed to the Sport category cars is over 62mph (100km/h), since the quicker 917LH reaches 224mph (360km/h). We only go up to 202mph (325km/h) with the short body and the 4.5-litre engine.

02:10

The alert sounds in the pit of the no.21 Porsche. The 917 driven by Siffert is coming in, with an idling engine and leaving behind it a trail of smoke. To everyone's surprise, he will retire with a broken engine, saying that in the previous lap he had missed a gearshift, causing a fatal overrev. All of a sudden, we are in the lead, but it's good to hold back the euphoria and not forget that we are not even at the halfway point in the race and that anything can happen! The 917 of Larrousse/Kauhsen is following us three laps behind.

I'm now next to the radio at home, tuned into shortwave, with the typical 'wheezing', as I turn the dial in search of the France Inter station, on the 39-metre band. I had remembered suddenly that this radio station used to broadcast short reporting notes on the main French sporting events and that I had listened to the reporting of the last Monte Carlo Rally in January. So I search anxiously to find the radio waves that might bring me information of what's happening at the de la Sarthe track. But it is not easy to find the right frequency; one must be patient and make several attempts, slowly turning the radio dial, then all of a sudden, there it is: *'Ici France Inter... nous rejoignons notre envoyé special au circuit des 24 Heures du Mans ... après dix heures de course'* [30] ... WIU ... WIUUU ... WIU ...'. As normal during these broadcasts the signal had been lost, so I have to turn the dial again smoothly until I pick it up once more (in the middle of many others that overlay each other): 'WIU ... WIU ... *La Porsche numéro 23 s'arrête maintenant à son stand... elle repart toujours en première position ...'.*[31]

Being both relieved and thankful, I tune into France Inter at the passing of every hour, since it is at the end of each news bulletin that the connection is established with the circuit. It's going to be a long night!

04:45

It is raining torrentially yet again and Kauhsen in the 'psychedelic' 917 no.3 is forced to stop with a flooded ignition, which causes engine failure.

06:10

The storm continues and the Sport cars are rolling between 5 and 6 minutes per lap. There are even some GTs that can pass them in certain areas of the circuit. We are still heroically in first position, followed by Elford two laps behind.

08:30

The rain has stopped, cars are speeding up once again, but 917 no.25 stops unexpectedly in the pit with an engine problem and retirement is inevitable. The beautiful 908 no.27 of Rudi Lins and Helmut Marko goes up to second position, but still three laps behind our precious lead, which we are determined to keep until the end. But the hours to come are the hardest ones, since the worry about a malfunction, which is always possible, continues to increase, and it is necessary to maintain our concentration, when fatigue is already a significant presence.

The 914/6 of Claude Ballot-Léna and Guy Chasseuil will win the GT category, finishing in an honourable sixth place in the overall standings.

10:00

Our lead increases to five laps due to problems in one of the 908's wheels, which make it lose time in the pit. Meanwhile, we pass a GT-class Porsche, the 914/6 no.40 of Guy Chasseuil/Claude Ballot-Léna that, with its small 2-litre engine, has maintained a titanic battle, like David and Goliath, with a 7-litre Chevrolet Corvette. Light weight and agility versus power and brute force.

12:00

We are still in the lead, when the rain hits us hard again, now five laps ahead of the 'psychedelic' 917, whose paint job is the work of Tony Lapine, designer for the brand.

15:00

We go into the last hour of racing with the hope of winning becoming more and more present, since our advantage is now six laps and the track is dry again.

15:22

Last pit stop. Our nervousness increases throughout the team. Ferry Porsche, Huschke von Hanstein, Ferdinand Piech and all the other Porsche staff look on anxiously but confidently, hoping for a happy ending. After refuelling we are off, with Herrmann still at the wheel. After so many years of dedication to the brand, he deserves more than any other the honour for the first time of taking a Porsche to the winning position at the 24 Hours of Le Mans. Each pass on the start/finish straight represents one more step, with Herrmann looking anxiously towards the official clock, which seems to run slower than ever!

The mighty 917 gives Porsche its first overall win at the 24 Hours of Le Mans.

16:00

When we finally come out of the Ford Chicane and go into the start/finish straight, Herrmann is expecting and hoping to see the chequered flag, but to his astonishment and almost desperation, the race director doesn't show it, and we're forced to do another lap, which, for the crowd, is already a celebration lap, clapping and waving flags. After the last 8.4 miles (13.49km) of the 2,863 miles (4,607km) done over the 24 hours, finally the win materializes. The joy of the Porsche clan is immense. Ferry Porsche rejoices and thinks of his father, of how he would be proud at this very special moment. To top off such a memorable day, the brand also wins the GT race with the 914/6 and also the prototype category with the 908/2 and all this in an extremely hard race in which only seven of the fifty-one cars finished, and from those seven, five are Porsches!

While the mechanics push the 917 to the parc fermé, I finally give in to the fatigue, falling into a comforting lethargy. I can only recall a few hours later being bumped around as I'm loaded into the transport truck headed to Stuttgart. There the reception is amazing. I cannot forget the commemorative parade for the win, done with dozens of Porsches behind the 917, through the streets of Stuttgart for the joy of its inhabitants and fans of the brand!

The 24 hours of Le Mans had become for Porsche the most important racing event since its first participation in 1951. It had managed many class wins over twenty years, but the big dream was overall victory and finally the dream came true in 1970 with a faultless race, excellent drivers and a fantastic car.

The 917 is undoubtedly a Porsche icon due to the dominance it achieved in the two full seasons (1970–1) in which it competed officially for the marque, and undoubtedly also due to its design, sound and astonishing performance. Of course, the fact that it gave Porsche its first overall victory in the 24 Hours of Le Mans was an important and significant milestone for the brand and for the fans.

The man behind the 917 project was Ferdinand Piech, who aspired to have a winning car in the new category created by FIA – Sport up to 5-litres, which could possibly finally give Porsche victory in the 24 Hours of Le Mans. The new regulations for this category required the manufacture of a minimum of twenty-five cars, which was a major challenge for Porsche. The new car was announced in May 1968 and ten months later was presented at the Geneva Motor Show. Porsche managed to develop the car in such a short time by using the 908 chassis as the basis for the project. Entirely new was the 12-cylinder engine with a 4.5-litre capacity. Hans Mezger and his team did an outstanding job, as the engine

Porsche 917s parade in Stuttgart celebrating the 24 Hours of Le Mans victory.

revealed from the outset its potential and endurance, quickly developing 580bhp after the first runs on the test bench.

The 917 was rolled out for the first time in public in the pre-practice of the 24 Hours of Le Mans on 29 March 1969. They were the first tests at high speeds, in which the 917 exceeded 200mph (320km/h), but the drivers (Herrmann, Stommelen and Ahrens) complained of not being able to use all the available engine power due to the car's instability at these speeds. Those handling and stability problems even caused some resistance by the drivers to race with the 917 in 1969, preferring often to use the 'old' 908. However, the Porsche 917 managed to gain its first victory in competition in the Austria 1,000km with Siffert/Ahrens. The problems were solved between the end of the 1969 season and the beginning of the 1970 Championship, when the 917 came up with aerodynamic changes primarily visible on the new short tail. The drivers soon found the value of the changes and the 917 quickly became a winner and the car to beat in all the races in which it competed.

They were indeed two years with many victories and fantastic races, which left an indelible and unique image on Porsche fans. Also the drivers who had the privilege of racing the 917 still recall those times with nostalgia, being unanimous in saying that it was the most fantastic car they had the opportunity to drive.

SEPTEMBER 1970, LE MANS, FRANCE

The Slate Grey 911 goes through a deserted road near Le Mans, its unique and irreproducible sound standing out in the rural environment. Its elegant silhouette goes by a lane of centenarian trees, the strategically placed cameras capturing the near idyllic moment of symbiosis of mechanics, design and nature. We are going across the L'Huisne river on a beautiful metallic bridge from where one can see the steeple of a church on the side of the road.

Steve McQueen is the driver of the 911 and he is filming the initial moments of the film Le Mans. *Despite being for a film, the moments are quite real and I can guess the pleasure McQueen is feeling, enjoying the quietness of the morning as he cruises among the fields of de la Sarthe. He is cradled by the sound of the engine and the glide of the car, which feels almost like an extension of his own body, as he moves the lever to shift down to go into a turn, then accelerates away on the power coming from the engine.*

We are now in the city of Le Mans, which awakes from its morning torpor. We go through the Place des Jacobins, which is so familiar to the drivers and enthusiasts that come to Le Mans to live through the 24 hours of the race, since it is here where every year the technical verifications and weighing of the cars is done. We stop at a traffic light, the engine purrs softly, Steve looks towards the flower shop, where a beautiful woman has just bought a bouquet of roses ...

This is in fact how the film, which became a classic for lovers of automobile sport in general and even more so for Porsche fans, starts. For me, since it was at this time that I started admiring the cars made by the Stuttgart brand, the film became something very special, seen over and over in cinemas and then at home, always captivating and magical. From those calm initial moments in which the 911 crosses the screen serenely, with a near ethereal beauty (thus becoming an object of desire) to the spectacular racing and circuit scenes, the film is a feast for the senses! The 907, 908, 911, 914 and 917 that parade before us in the scenes allow us also to experience the unique environment of the de la Sarthe circuit.

The Porsche 908 of Herbert Linge and Jonathan Williams fitted with 70mm filming cameras before the start of the 1970 24 Hours of Le Mans.

The 908/2 belonging to Steve McQueen and engaged by Solar Productions achieved its main purpose of recording fantastic shots for the film *Le Mans*.

During the race held in June 1970, the 908 driven by Herbert Linge and Jonathan Williams, which carried two cameras, completed the entire race, getting spectacular images for the film and only failing to finish in the top ten because it had not driven the minimum distance, missing 63 miles (102km), as it was penalized by the additional pit stops to change the film rolls.

Steve McQueen himself wanted to participate in the race, but the insurance companies would not allow it. He was completely committed to the film, acting in most of the scenes himself and only being replaced by a stuntman in the most dangerous accident shots.

The filming went on for several weeks at the 24-hour circuit and besides the large number of cars bought and rented for the production, a great number of highly regarded drivers were part of the team,

Steve McQueen in the paddock of Le Mans circuit with the famous Slate Grey 911 S he used as his personal car while he was at Le Mans and that is also the 'star' of the first scenes of the *Le Mans* film.

Some of the 917s used in *Le Mans* during a break in filming.

Steve McQueen relaxes before returning to action as 'Michael Delaney' in *Le Mans.*

with one of them, David Piper, having lost a leg as the result of a crash. Undoubtedly the film *Le Mans* remains one of the greatest performances by Steve McQueen who was a man passionate about racing – 'Racing is life. Anything before or after is just waiting.'

17–18 APRIL 1971, CIRCUIT DE LA SARTHE, LE MANS, FRANCE

It is usual that, two months before the running of the 24 Hours of Le Mans, there is a weekend of preliminary testing, so that the manufacturers can test the solutions they think will suit the unique track that is the de la Sarthe circuit. Porsche has brought several 917s and has as its main objective testing the aerodynamic changes in the Long Tail 917LH and also to validate a new variant, the 917/20, which is wider than the normal version (62.4in/1,600mm). All the changes were made planning for the maximum speed possible on the famous Hunaudières Straight, without too much compromise of performance in other areas of the circuit. It is said that it will be possible to reach speeds well above 230mph (370km/h)!

I could not resist this challenge and I will certainly witness many interesting moments on chassis no.043, a LH (Long Tail) version, whose body, painted in an immaculate white, carries the number 21. During the weekend several drivers will take their place behind its wheel, in an attempt to beat the record of the previous year, when in the practice for the June race, the 917LH of Vic Elford achieved 3min 19.8sec.

The Porsche 917LH at Le Mans 1971 April tests, where it showed its fantastic top speed at the Hunaudières Straight.

On this late Saturday morning, Jo Siffert is at the wheel, determined to achieve a good time. We take the Tertre Rouge turn with the best possible trajectory so that we go into the Hunaudières at maximum speed, then we accelerate and hope that no slower car shows up to compromise the lap. Siffert's concentration is at maximum, because driving at over 217mph (350km/h) on a road that is not very wide and is flanked by trees demands it, especially as the wind can destabilize a car at these speeds when you least expect it. We are probably going at 230mph (370km/h) and the 'hill' at the end of the straight is already approaching. We must be very alert for this and the subsequent braking at the Mulsanne corner. Next we go up again to speeds nearing 217mph (350km/h) until the first Indianapolis turn. Siffert takes several laps in sequence and successively gets 3min 18.4sec, 3min 18.2sec, 3min 18sec and finally 3min 17sec before stopping. He then leaves to catch the plane to Barcelona, where he is going to take part in the Spanish Formula One Grand Prix.

On Sunday morning around 09:00, Jackie Oliver sits down in the 917 no.21, since he wants to take advantage while there is no wind in order to establish the best time of the weekend. The times go down rapidly: 3min 16.9sec, 3min 16sec, 3min 15sec and around 10:00h a fantastic 3min 13.6sec! Without a doubt, these

Porsche 917LH and 917/20 at Arnage curve during April tests in Le Mans (1971).

Porsche 917 K no.22 of Helmut Marko and Gijs van Lennep after the start of 1971 24 Hours of Le Mans in front of a Ferrari 512 S and Porsche 917/20 no.23 of Willi Kauhsen and Reinhold Jöst.

Porsche 917 K no.22 is refuelled during a pit stop near the end of the 1971 24 Hours of Le Mans.

last 3 minutes were some of the most extraordinary that I have lived through until today. For the first time in the history of the circuit, a car has done a lap with an average speed over 155.4mph (250km/h), 155.634mph (250.457km/h) to be precise.

We've just stopped in the pits, the results are announced and the spectators applaud, thrilled and astonished at such a feat. Without a doubt, these tests at the de la Sarthe circuit have been gratifying for everyone and are a large incentive for Porsche's competition department, whose expectations to achieve a second victory in the race have been reinforced.

The victorious 917 K established a distance record in the 24 Hours of Le Mans that would not be broken for thirty-nine years.

On the race of 12 and 13 June, Porsche confirmed the advantage attributed to it after the tests in April, dominating the race completely and maintaining the lead throughout almost all the race, except for a period of less than 1 hour during the night. Victory ended up going to a 917 K enrolled by Martini Racing and driven by Helmut Marko and Gijs Van Lennep, who, while not being the fastest, had a very regular race without any major problems. They stopped a planned twenty-eight times, totalling 51 minutes in the pits for refuelling and changing tyres, with only two unexpected stops to replace the alternator belt and to fasten the cool-

ing fan of the engine. Even so, they beat the record of distance driven, which had been in place since 1967 (in a Ford MK IV driven by Dan Gurney and A.J. Foyt), by driving 3,315.7 miles (5,335km) in the 24 hours at an average of 138.1mph (222.3km/h).[32]

The 917 no.22 (chassis 053) had the uniqueness of being built in magnesium, a material even lighter than aluminium and also a lot more expensive. Porsche had decided to experiment with this material, always showing a commitment to innovation in the search for better performance, rather than achieving it solely by increasing the power of the engines.

Porsche not only got its second victory in the 24 Hours, but also ended up winning the World Championship for Makes for the fourth consecutive year. Porsche's domination started to 'bother' a lot of people, in such a way that the authorities for automotive sport decided to end the Sport category from 1972, making it impossible for Porsche to participate any more with its amazing 917. This decision by the FIA would have repercussions for the marque's strategy, causing it to turn towards the USA instead and developing the 917 even further so as to be able to participate in the Can-Am Championship, which had great prestige in the American continent and whose popularity was also starting to reach Europe.

15 OCTOBER 1972, LAGUNA SECA, USA

The eighth race in the Can-Am Championship of 1972 is about to end and 47,000 spectators are distributed along the well-known Californian circuit of Laguna Seca. In the lead is the Porsche 917/10 no.7 (chassis 10/003) of George Follmer. The 1,000bhp of the flat-12 engine is about to give us a serious 'kick' as we exit the left turn, which precedes the run-up to the famous Corkscrew corner, projecting us, like a bullet out of a Winchester rifle, at a speed to which the cars of the other brands cannot aspire. We brake sharply in order to navigate this challenging curve, then descend towards the finish line. Follmer takes what's left of the lap cautiously, since he does not want to miss the opportunity of making history in this popular American championship. And that is what happens, when we drive across the finish line – George Follmer has just become champion, making Porsche the winner too and ending the domination of the American brands Lola and McLaren since 1966.

There is still one race to go before the end of the championship, but the domination of Porsche so far (six wins in nine races) allows for this early celebration. It has been a lively championship, in which I have had a lot of fun in all the races, enjoying the extraordinary performance of the most powerful competition car Porsche has built to date. It was gratifying as well to watch the confirmation of

George Follmer drives the 917/10 to victory at Laguna Seca and to the 1972 Can-Am Championship title.

an excellent driver, George Follmer, who managed to make us forget the absence of the renowned Mark Donohue, who could not participate in five races due to an accident. I can hardly wait for the last race, which will be a well-deserved celebration, but I especially look forward to next year's Championship, which promises even more good news and to be even more spectacular!

With its forced move to the American races, Porsche ended up with a good pay-off from challenging the until then uncontested McLaren, getting a result that was as overwhelming as it was unexpected, at least for the Americans. This success was due not only to the technology adopted, but also to the excellent organizational capability and the partnership strategy with a renowned American team, led by Roger Penske.

As for the technical factors, one must highlight the use of turbochargers to feed the already powerful flat-12 of the 917. And this was no easy task, since some innovation was necessary to be able to reduce to an acceptable minimum the so-called 'turbo lag', without which the driving would become practically impossible. Mark Donohue, who was a mechanical engineer as well as an excellent driver, undoubtedly played an important role in the development and testing of the technical solutions that were found. It became possible to reach 1,000bhp, while maintaining the necessary reliability to be able to defeat the robust 800bhp V8 Chevrolet engines that equipped the McLarens.

All this development implied many work hours in the engine department in Weissach, led by Hans Mezger. Everything that Porsche conceived and tested was innovative, since no other marque had decided to attack the problem of the response time for turbocharged engines in such a thorough and demanding way. There was no way to calculate precisely the results that could be obtained according to each solution that was applied. Thus it was a job of 'learning by doing', consuming a

Georges Follmer with the Porsche 917/10 at Watkins Glen Can-Am race (1972).

lot of work hours and dedication. But it was worth it because with this acquired knowledge the brand was not only able to achieve its immediate objectives in competition, but also it would soon prove possible to incorporate the new technology into series production engines, which would bring much prestige to Porsche. By winning the Can-Am Championship, which was so dear to the Americans, Porsche reinforced its already good image on the continent, boosting its sales in the process and making the market even more important for the Stuttgart make.

3–4 FEBRUARY 1973, DAYTONA, USA

The 24 Hours of Daytona is the first race of the World Sportscar Championship, reserved for Sport-Prototypes and GTs. After the exclusion of the 5-litre sports cars at the end of 1971, Porsche stopped participating officially in this championship, turning to the Can-Am Championship that it dominated in 1972, through Roger Penske's team and its drivers Mark Donohue and George Follmer. Roger Penske has decided to take advantage of the opportunity to give some competitive practice to his drivers using the new weapon of the Stuttgart make, the 911 Carrera RSR. It is an evolution of the 911 Carrera RS, presented at the 1972 Paris Auto Show, with it being announced that only 500 units would be produced, the minimum number to obtain homologation in that category.

The initial test will be at this race, with two works supported cars, one for the Penske team and another for the Brumos Racing team, also an already frequent user in the USA of Porsche racing cars, besides its business representing and selling the German cars. With the short amount of time between the presentation of the Carrera RS and the race at Daytona, the cars aren't homologated in the GT category yet, so they will race integrated in the Sport-Prototype group when

The new Porsche 911 Carrera RSR (no.59) of Peter Gregg and Hurley Haywood at Daytona Speedway during the 24-hour race (1973).

it comes to standings. This situation does not really matter for Porsche, since the objective is to test the potential and endurance of the new machine.

The engine is an evolution of the one that will be commercialized in the 'client' version, since it has had its displacement increased from 2700cc to 2806cc, going from 210bhp to about 300bhp. The suspension has also been changed and the brakes have been imported from the 917. Porsche knows it has almost no chance of winning at Daytona, as the race is usually fought amongst the Sport cars, represented by two Mirage M6s (of John Wyer's team), a Matra 670, a Lola 282, two Porsche 908s and one 910 that are privately owned, three Chevrons and a Lotus. With my previous 'connection' to the team of Roger Penske at the Can-Am races of last year, I'm naturally 'settled' in the beautiful Carrera RSR no.6 painted in the blue colour of the main sponsor, Sunoco.

The other Carrera RSR of the Brumos team, which will be driven by Hurley Haywood and Peter Gregg, is painted in the traditional colours of the team, white with blue and red stripes, while also bearing its talisman number, 59. In the qualifying practice our car had some problems and we only finished twelfth, though this appears to be a normal position behind the cars in the Sport category. But the surprise came from the other Carrera RSR, which got a magnificent eighth place on the grid (despite being more than 16 seconds behind the first, which was the Mirage of Derek Bell and Howden Ganley), taking advantage of some mechanical problems that the more powerful competitors were experiencing. In the Porsche no.6, it is Mark Donohue who is going to start the race, in the traditional American running-start behind the pace car. When it leaves the track and sets the race cars free, we find ourselves in the middle of the Chevrolet Corvettes and Camaros, which form a major part of the starting grid.

The lead is taken by the Mirage of Mike Hailwood, followed by the Matra of François Cévert and by the other Mirage of Derek Bell. During the first lap, Donohue has to make an unscheduled stop in the pits to check the tyres and we lose some places. The Carrera RSR no.59 is driving in front of the pack of GTs, the ones that really matter in terms of comparative performance. From the second hour, problems start to arise in the front-running cars, when Derek Bell's Mirage and Jean-Louis Lafosse's Lola stop with ignition problems and lose some laps.

We're now recovering the lost time by forcing our pace a bit more, since the rivalry between the Brumos and Penske team demands it. In front, Jean-Pierre Beltoise in the Matra 670 goes briefly into the lead when Mike Hailwood is forced to stop to fix a panel of the bodywork on his car. But the Matra isn't going to push it and the Mirage quickly gets back in the lead. Then the Mirage is forced to make a long stop to replace the clutch and the same happens to the other car in the team. The remaining cars in the Sport category are also experiencing problems and suddenly and unexpectedly the two Carrera RSRs find themselves in second and third place, behind the Matra of Cévert/Beltoise, which has a ten-

lap lead. Thus we are behind the no.59 of Gregg/Haywood and we have also a ten-lap lead over the best Corvette chasing us.

It is almost midnight when new theatrics happen. Cévert, in the leading Matra, stops at the entrance to the banking, with a broken engine. After 10 hours of racing, the two 'beginner' Carrera RSRs are now in the first two positions! Will they endure the 14 hours of racing still ahead? Now that the battle is between the two rival American teams, both will do whatever is possible to get in the lead. The headlights sweep the night, slamming into the banking as we exit the road part of the circuit. The engine is pushed to near its limit on this slanted part of the track. It screams with its characteristic growl as the rpm needle revs close to the red line for 2 miles (3km), testing the engine's endurance to the maximum.

Is it wise to continue this duel, which may turn into fratricide? Unfortunately, it is our engine that gives out first and by the fifteenth hour we have been forced to retire with a problem in a connecting rod, much to Donohue's and Follmer's dismay. Gregg and Haywood are now less pressured and are able to relax a bit, since they have a considerable lead over the pursuers and the quicker Sport cars are all out of the race.

Brumo's team manages to keep its lead until the end of the race, resulting in an unexpected win, and in a car derived from a series production model, the 911 Carrera RS. There are celebrations at Daytona, but also in Stuttgart, with this victorious baptism showing such promise for the brand's new model.[33]

Porsche achieves an unexpected win at the 1973 24 Hours of Daytona with the Carrera RSR beating much more powerful opponents.

The victory achieved here was just the first indication of the enormous success that the Carrera RS would come to have, not only in competition, but also in its commercial version. The factory, which had expected only to produce the 500 units necessary for homologation, ended up making 1,580, which quickly sold out. The car's success was due not only to the prestige of the brand, but also to its innovative rear 'duck tail' aileron, reduced weight and promised performance due to its extraordinary engine. It became one of Porsche's greatest icons, representing its extraordinary concentrated 'DNA'!

28 OCTOBER 1973, RIVERSIDE RACEWAY, USA

On this last Sunday of October there is a lot of excitement at the Riverside circuit. The crowd attending have come not only to see the race of the Can-Am Championship, but also because of the new mini-championship called IROC (International Race of Champions), which gathers together some of the best drivers in current times to compete in identical cars that have been exclusively prepared for this goal, the Porsche 911 RSR.

The warm-up lap for the third race planned for this weekend at Riverside is now under way and Mark Donohue is starting from the first row of the grid with his no.12 Porsche. The dozen cars follow the pace car, a 914, and get ready to start. The 911s form a colourful bunch, each one in its striking colours with the name of the drivers (and what a set of drivers it is!) glued to the windshields: Emerson Fittipaldi; Mark Donohue; Peter Revson; George Follmer; David Pearson; Dennis Hulme; Bobby Unser; A.J. Foyt; Bobby Allinson; Richard Petty; Gordon Johncock;

The twelve famous drivers of the Porsche Carrera RSR in the IROC wait behind the pace car for the moment to speed up and fight for victory at the Riverside circuit.

and Roger McCluskey. The drivers selected are among the best from Formula One, NASCAR, Indy and the Can-Am Championships.

The race will go for thirty laps around the 2.48-mile (4km) circuit and I'm sure that Donohue, who has been very committed throughout the weekend and has won the first race, will give me more moments of pure enjoyment with the 911 RSR. The pace car releases the pack, Donohue puts his foot down and off we go, followed closely by McCluskey, Petty, Johncock and Hulme.

Even though the circuit is fast it has some tighter corners and we must be careful because going off the track implies a great loss of time in the dirt run-off areas. Donohue is managing to keep the lead, but Hulme is closing quickly. We are keeping a lively duel with him until the twenty-third lap, in which he makes a mistake and spins, losing several places. The thirtieth and final lap confirms Donohue's victory, followed by Unser, Fittipaldi and Revson. Donohue is thrilled because he has achieved his goal and is leaving Riverside with two wins and in the third position of the new Championship with twenty-five points, just four away from the leaders, Follmer and Unser, who have twenty-nine. He is now in a good place to fight for the title in the last race, which will be held at Daytona in February 1974.

But the fun and thrills aren't over yet, since in the afternoon the second to last race of the Can-Am Championship will be run and Donohue will certainly fight for the title with the fabulous 917/30. After a great battle with Follmer in a 917/10, Donohue manages to get the win when Follmer has to retire with a *mechanical problem. This does not take away from the merit of the win, since Donohue has already won five of the seven races. With this sixth victory, Donohue rejoices after a spectacular season for him and for Porsche, which, with the 917/30 and its 1,100bhp, has tested both the skill and ability of the driver, but also the car's endurance in the face of technical challenges.*

And for me it has been a fantastic season, experiencing passion and excitement in a near 'otherworldly' car like the 917/30 and in the 911 RSR at the IROC Championship.

The idea for the creation of the IROC Championship came from team owner Roger Penske and Les Richter, president of the Riverside Raceway. The objective, even if it was somewhat theoretical, was to celebrate the best racing driver in the world, by inviting the most outstanding drivers in Europe and America to run several races in cars that were as identical as possible. Penske and Richter came up with the ideal number of twelve drivers to contend a four-race championship, with the support of the ABC network, which would broadcast the races.

The first difficulty they came across was choosing the car, since it would have to be quite powerful, robust and easy to maintain. Of course, for Roger Penske, who had been working with Porsche since 1972, the choice of the marque was obvious and the model that he had in mind was the 911 Carrera RSR, which his team had just used in the 24 Hours of Daytona. The biggest doubt was whether the competition department at

A colourful 'palette' of Carrera RSRs at Zuffenhausen factory ready to depart for the USA, where they will race in the new IROC Championship.

Zuffenhausen would be able to supply the fifteen cars (twelve plus three reserves) in a relatively short amount of time. The answer was affirmative and it was guaranteed that they would be supplied with rigorously identical specifications, except in colours, since each car would have its own. And in fact the big surprise when the cars were seen for the first time on the patio of the factory in Zuffenhausen, before being sent to the United States, was the wide and flashy range of colours they showcased.

Each car cost $25,000 and came ready to race, with a 3-litre engine emitting 316bhp and tuned in such a way that the maximum differential among the cars was no more than 2bhp. They were equipped with a roll bar, the fenders were those of the RS 3.0, narrower so that the car would more closely resemble the series version, and the rims were fixed with the traditional five bolts instead of the centre lock. They also came equipped with the drilled brake discs of the 917 and all the cars were checked as to their final weight. Another particularity was the fact that the cars had left the factory with the original rear hood of the Carrera RS, known as the 'ducktail', but it was replaced before the first race by the 'tea tray' rear hood of the 911 turbo.

The rules that the races would follow would also be quite innovative, with the objective of ensuring as much as possible the same conditions for all the drivers. So, after each race all the drivers switched cars, with the winner going to the last-place car for the next race, the second finisher using the second to last and so on for all the others. The money prizes were attractive, with the winner taking home more than $50,000.

Mark Donohue wins the IROC Championship after his victory in the last and spectacular race at Daytona.

The races were a success, both for the drivers involved and also for the audience. The win in the Championship ended up going to Mark Donohue, who won two of the three races fought on the weekend at Riverside, plus the last one at Daytona in February 1974. This latter was a fantastic race, with a spectacular battle between Donohue, Peter Revson, David Pearson and George Follmer, who finished the race and the Championship in this order.

The 911 RSRs were then sold and continued to win races in the hands of many private drivers and to this day some of them compete in classic race events in the United States. They were in fact a unique 'species', due mostly to their particularities, but also due to the fact of having been driven enthusiastically by some of the best drivers in the world!

But that weekend at Riverside was specially marked by the win in the race and in the Can-Am Championship for Mark Donohue with the fabulous 917/30. This incredible machine was the evolution of the 917/10, which had won the Championship in the previous year with George Follmer, but it had even more power, with its unbelievable 1,100bhp. And Donohue was the right driver, as he could live up to such a demanding machine, proving it by winning six of the eight races of the Championship.

The supremacy of the turbo technology by Porsche was once again proved and the 917/30 was imprinted on the memory of an entire generation of spectators who had the opportunity to see and hear it on the American race tracks. To this day, it is the centre of attention at any meeting or classic car race in which it takes part and even the current drivers who get a chance to drive it are amazed by the capabilities and performance of this machine that is over forty years old.

The Porsche 917/30 with 1,100bhp was the most powerful Porsche ever made and Mark Donohue drove it with extreme skill to dominate the 1973 Can-Am Championship.

12 JUNE 1977, CIRCUIT DE LA SARTHE, LE MANS, FRANCE

It is 15:45 and there are only 15 minutes until the end of the forty-fifth running of the 24 Hours of Le Mans. The Porsche 936 no.4, which has been leading the race since 10:00, has been stopped in the pits for half an hour, due to problems in one of the cylinders of the flat-6. It's the no.3 cylinder on the right side of the engine and the mechanics, taking into account the seventeen-lap lead that the 936 has over the second-place runner, the Mirage of Vern Schuppan and Jean-Pierre Jarier, have decided to disconnect the ignition and fuel supply to that cylinder, to allow the engine to do the last two laps that the regulations demand, so that they can claim Porsche's fourth victory at the de la Sarthe circuit.

Curiously, the mechanics ended up attaching a big watch to the steering wheel so that Jürgen Barth, the engineer-driver who will have the hard task of bringing the car to the finish line, can control the exact timing in which he should perform the two laps before seeing the chequered flag. The emotions in the Porsche pit are at their peak, and everyone is anxiously awaiting the final result, especially Jacky Ickx and Hurley Haywood, the other two drivers of the no.4 car.

The race so far has not been easy for the Stuttgart cars, since the 'sister' car, the no.3 of Henri Pescarolo and Jacky Ickx, has been forced to retire prematurely during the fourth hour of racing. Before that, the 936 no.4 lost a lot of time in

Jürgen Barth waits for the order to go to the track and drive the 'wounded' 936 to the fourth Porsche victory at the 24 Hours of Le Mans.

the pits when it had to have its injection pump replaced. It went down from third to forty-first and lost nine laps. Porsche's racing management decided, after the withdrawal of the no.3 car, to put Jacky Ickx in the no.4, and that's how the Belgian driver, taking advantage of the rain and the wet track, managed to perform a spectacular recovery through the night, taking the 936 to second place by 05:00.

The 936, after some initial problems, made an impressive recovery during the night when Jacky Ickx performed an astonishing drive in difficult heavy rain conditions.

They were several consecutive hours of superb driving, very fast but safe, a driving show that I shall never forget. At that time, the Alpine-Renault of Jean-Pierre Jabouille and Derek Bell was in the lead, but it would be forced to retire at the end of the seventh hour with engine problems, thus allowing the Porsche to jump into the lead. But now, everything is at stake again and it is necessary to endure two more laps to be able to celebrate victory.

The watch on the steering wheel of the 936 is now showing 15:50 and Barth gets the order to go, which he does as carefully as possible, leaving behind a small trail of white smoke, a clear sign of the engine problem. We've already gone under the Dunlop Bridge towards the Esses turn and a bit later we're at Tertre Rouge. We are now on the Hunaudières, driving at a much slower speed than usual and the straight now seems longer than ever. Barth is listening for any strange noises emanating from the engine and he's handling the mechanics 'with kid gloves'.

We pass Mulsanne, Indianapolis, Arnage and everything seems to be fine, with Barth not going over 4,000rpm. We go into the Ford Chicane and through the start/finish line at 15:56, but there is still another lap to go, which will be one of even greater expectation and anxiety. Barth continues driving carefully, without any major problems, and we go through the finish line 2 minutes after 16:00, to the great joy and excitement of the Porsche team. It is without doubt a memorable race, filled with suspense, but which gave way to another fabulous victory for Porsche!

The Porsche 936 had started competing in 1976 and gave the marque victory in the World Sportscar Championship by winning all six races, including the 24 Hours of Le Mans with Jacky Ickx and Gijs van Lennep.

Jürgen Barth finishes the 24-hour race after two final thrilling laps, giving his teammates (Ickx and Haywood) and Porsche one more victory at Le Mans.

Porsche also won in 1976 the World Championship for Makes with the 935. So it was a season that allowed for wins on two fronts, taking advantage of the fact that the FIA had created two separate championships.

The 936 made use of the knowledge acquired with the 917 and the 908/3 in terms of chassis and engine, even though the regulations limited the size of the engines to 2.1-litres for turbocharged engines and 3-litres for atmospheric ones. Porsche benefited from all the know-how in this area, having developed the 917 previously and then the 934 and 935. These last two had the same engine, but with a displacement of 2.8-litres and 520bhp for the 936 and over 600bhp for the 935. Only three chassis of the 936 were made, but even so their number of victories was significant, highlighted by the three victories in the 24 Hours of Le Mans.[34]

23–27 MARCH 1978, KENYA

The East African Safari is one of the most exciting and toughest races in the World Rally Championship. It's made up of almost 2,921 miles (4,700km) of African dirt tracks, laden with traps, to be driven by the contenders at a hellish pace for five days. The cars have to be prepared specially for this race, reinforcing the chassis and the suspension, increasing the distance to the ground, setting up protection against possible 'encounters' with the local fauna, using special exhausts that allow for the crossing of streams and reducing engine power; in fact, trying in any way to anticipate the difficulties that cannot be avoided during this extremely difficult route.

The two 911 SC factory cars engaged in the 1978 East African Safari, no.14 for Preston/ Lyall and no.5 for Waldegård/ Thorszelius.

Porsche is striving for the victory that is missing from the gallery of this most charismatic of events, which it almost won in 1974, until Björn Waldegård unfortunately had to retire while leading the race comfortably, with the finish almost in sight. It is a heavy bet that Porsche is making, bringing two 911 SCs for Waldegård/Hans Thorszelius and Vic Preston/John Lyall. The specially prepared cars have an engine that generates 250bhp for its 2,604lb (1,180kg) weight, and reaches a top speed of 130.5mph (210km/h). 12,430 miles (20,000km) of 'in loco' testing have been carried out and the support team has eight vehicles, one aeroplane and twenty-five mechanics led by a respected staff, including Peter Falk, Manfred Jankte and Jürgen Barth.

All the stages depart and arrive in Nairobi. The first one is played out along 1,136 miles (1,829km) over 27 hours. On this Thursday, 23 March, it is almost 14:00, with the start time getting closer under a heavy sky. Björn Waldegård, in the 911 SC no.5, is ready to start the race, calm and relaxed, since he has a large amount of experience in this rally, unlike others who are discovering the African event for the first time.

At the top of the starting ramp, I enjoy my privileged 'workstation', from where I can see the row of supplementary headlights at the end of the hood and the protection bars for encounters with wild animals. After the start we set off towards Nakuru, along the typically African roads, made of rough dirt with the additional menace of potholes and bumps that can easily break the suspension. In Nakuru, land of the pink flamingos, there is only one team without penalties, Vic Preston in the other 911 SC.

After this point Waldegård attacks heavily and before the halfway point on the stage we're leading the race, despite the difficulties experienced in the mud flats in the most northern zone of the stage. We return to Nairobi on Friday, already past 17:00, and even though we have 153 penalty points (corresponding to 2hr 33min) we are in first place in the standings, with a 45-minute lead over the Datsun of Rauno Aaltonen and Harry Kallstrom. Vic Preston in the 911 no.14

2,921 miles (4,700km) of African roads justify why the East African Safari was the toughest rally in its time.

A brief pause for the 911 SCs and their drivers during the 1978 East African Safari.

has gone down to seventh position, with a 57-minute delay. One has to take maximum advantage of the few rest hours, since the departure for the second leg will be at around 06:00 on Saturday.

This stage, with a length of 1,063 miles (1,711km), is difficult and Waldegård is keen to hang on to the lead he achieved in the first stage. We are now in the Taita Hills area, when suddenly the 911 slides as we exit a turn, the rear skids and we hear a bang as the rear axle hits a bump in the road. Waldegård stops immediately, gets out of the car and inspects the damage with Thorszelius. The diagnosis is not good – a broken suspension. We have to wait for assistance to do the repair, so by the next control point in Mombasa we have fallen to seventh place, 37 minutes behind the Datsun of Aaltonen.

But the adversities do not stop here. During the night-time return to Nairobi, a broken shock absorber has to be replaced by Waldegård, with Thorszelius illuminating the scene with a flashlight. Then a puncture contributes to further delay, which at the end of this leg is 47 minutes, corresponding to sixth place in the standings. Waldegård is disappointed, because even though he has already won the Safari, he would like to do it again in a Porsche, but it seems that this still won't be his year. The other car of the team is in third place, 19 minutes away from the leader, the Datsun of Aaltonen.

Waldegård still hasn't thrown in the towel and he sets off on the attack for the last stage (715 miles/1,151km), which takes place between Easter Sunday and Monday. In the first 124 miles (200km) we are able to recover 10 minutes, but 50 miles (80km) further ahead bad luck strikes again – a drive shaft gives in, victim to another bump in the road. This is the Safari, rough and unpredictable, and Waldegård now knows for sure that it won't be this time that he'll give Porsche a win in the African race.

However, after the repair, Waldegård is on the go again at a good pace and we finish the race in Nairobi in fourth place, contributing despite everything to a good team result by Porsche, since Vic Preston, after the retirement of the two official Datsuns, has finished in an honourable second place. Even though it isn't the desired win, this is a good result for the make, in this difficult race of the World Rally Championship.

As for me, after 3,107 miles (5,000km) of African 'roads' and adventures I am rather shaken up, but the experience in a race different from all the others in the Championship has been well worth it!

At the end of this rally, the result took Porsche to first place in the World Championship, since this year it had achieved another brilliant victory at the Monte Carlo Rally with the Jean-Pierre Nicolas/Vincent Laverne team, also in a 911 SC.

Porsche would never win the Safari, since in the following years it focused exclusively on circuit races. Curiously, Waldegård would win the 2011 edition of the 'classic' version of the rally, with a Porsche 911, accompanied by his son Mathias. This was one of the last races of the great champion, who, at sixty-seven years of age, finally made this old dream come true, taking a Porsche to a win in a race, which, even though it was not as hard as the original version, was still a great challenge for men and machines.

19–20 JUNE 1982, CIRCUIT DE LA SARTHE, LE MANS, FRANCE

The de la Sarthe circuit has once again come to life with the annual 24 Hours of Le Mans. This year, there are some big changes to the regulations of the types of cars allowed and also limitations placed on fuel consumption. The cars that are candidates for the overall victory are now included in group C, and Porsche has built a new car, the 956, according to the new regulations, hence it is a closed car with an aluminium monocoque, weighing around 1,854lb (840kg). With fluid lines, its aerodynamics are one of its main assets; for the first time in a Porsche the 'ground effect' is used, even if just partially. The engine is of the same type that was used in the previous year in the 936 that was victorious here at Le Mans, a flat-6, with 2.65-litre capacity and water-cooled 4-valve cylinder heads, putting out 620bhp.

The biggest problem that the technicians had to solve was the issue of consumption, since the new regulations demand that it must be below 5.65mpg (50ltr/100km), and with the limitation at Le Mans set at 572gal (2,600ltr) per car for the entire race and also the maximum volume allowed for the tank and tubing set at 22gal (100ltr). This is the main problem, not only for Porsche, but also for all the other contestants in group C, namely Rondeau, March, Lola, Ford and Sauber.

The Porsche team with the three 956s for the 1982 24 Hours of Le Mans stands for the 'family' photo at the Place des Jacobins in Le Mans, where, as usual, the ACO does the weighing and technical verifications of the cars.

Porsche has brought three 956s to Le Mans, to which the race numbers 1, 2 and 3 have been attributed to the teams of Jacky Ickx/Derek Bell, Jochen Mass/Vern Schuppan and Hurley Haywood/Al Holbert/Jürgen Barth, respectively. The practice sessions have gone normally and the Porsches nos 1 and 2 have easily conquered the first line of the starting grid, with Ickx lapping in 3min 28.4sec, an improvement by 1 second on his time of the previous year.

The 956s clearly dominated the race with no.1 (Ickx/Bell) leading the pack.

It's almost 15:00 on Saturday and the thousands of spectators in the stands are anxiously waiting for the start of the race. Ickx looks at the pace car that is about to start the warm-up lap and, as soon as it goes, he shifts into first gear and we go forth for another Porsche adventure! At the end of the warm-up lap, the pace car heads into the pit lane. The cars hold formation almost until the end of the start/finish straight, until the French flag is lowered, and that's when the brutal acceleration throws us into the first lap of the race. Jochen Mass in the no.2 car pushes a bit more and takes the lead, with us a few metres away.

Night-time at the de la Sarthe circuit is always magical, both on and off the track, with the powerful headlights of the cars sweeping the road, but also with all the commotion at *the fair that is set up next to the circuit, where many of the spectators have some fun, waiting for the sun to come up, when they will once again turn their attention to the race. The well-lit Ferris wheel near the Esses always offers a beautiful image as we pass it each lap and the spectators surely enjoy a fine view when they are at its top. For the team of the no.1 956, which is also at the top of the standings, everything is going well, in part because some small problems in the sister cars, no.2 (ignition) and no.3 (replacing a door), have contributed to solidifying the lead.*

All the Porsche team is longing for the seventh win at Le Mans with the 956's debut. During the final refuelling stop, Peter Falk gives his final instructions to Jacky Ickx and soon we're on the last lap, having already passed the Maison Blanche zone and coming up to the first Ford Chicane. Ickx is looking at the rear-view mirror to make sure that

The Porsche 'armada' is already in close formation near the end of the 24-hour race.

the nos 2 and 3 cars are following us closely behind, so that we can finish the race together in the same order as the standings, a manifestation of the superiority shown during the entire race. The marshals, as is tradition, come to the limit of the track waving their flags and the enthusiastic audience, which has invaded the area of the finish straight and the Ford Chicane, forces Ickx to slow down and we finish the race at walking pace, after having completed 359 laps and 3,044.7 miles (4,899km). It is a fantastic ending to a fantastic race!

The 1982 24 Hours of Le Mans were set into the history of the event as a famous victory for Porsche, since it not only achieved the first five places in the general standings, with the three 956s followed by two 935s, but it also won all the classes in the race:

- Group C: 956 (Ickx/Bell)
- Group GTC: 935 (Fitzpatrick/Hobbs)
- IMSA GTX: 935 (Snobeck/Servanin/Metge)
- IMSA GTO: 924 GTR (Busby/Bundy)
- Group V: 935 K3 (Cooper/Smith/Bourgoignie).

The overall winning 956 also got the 'Energy Efficiency' classification, with a consumption of 5.91mpg (47.79ltr/100km).

It is worth highlighting that of the eighteen cars in the standings by the end of the race, 50 per cent were Porsches! With this victory, a new period of domination in the 24 Hours of Le Mans began, through the 956 and its evolution, the 962, which together would obtain six consecutive victories. The main creators of these victories, beyond the drivers naturally, were men like Norbert Singer, responsible for the development of the chassis, Hans Mezger, responsible for the development of the engines, Klaus Bischoff, chief of mechanics, and Peter Falk, racing director, besides many others, either working at the factory or at the tracks, who gave their best towards the success of the marque.

22 JANUARY 1986, DAKAR, SENEGAL

There are a little more than 12.4 miles (20km) left in the 8,479-mile (13,643km) race that connects Paris to Dakar, most of them driven in the African territory. We're close to the Atlantic, on the immense beach that goes all the way to Dakar and our no.186 Porsche 959 is about to start this last timed sector, where all of the 530 starting drivers dream about arriving after three weeks of the hardest road race on the planet.

After the motorcycles start, we await the signal for the always spectacular simultaneous departure of the cars, in rows of three. René Metge is at the wheel and Dominique Lemoyne by his side, both confident in the win, which is now so close. Metge looks to his side and sees his sister car, no.185 of Jacky Ickx/Claude Brasseur, also ready to get going towards this legendary ending on the beaches of Senegal. The starting signal is given and here we go wishing to get to the end of this great 'raid' of the 20th century as quickly as possible.

The Mitsubishi Pajero of Rigal/Maingret, which is in third place in the standings behind Ickx's 959, gets ahead a bit, but the 959 drivers aren't taking the bait, since the positions are perfectly defined and the Mitsubishi is almost 5 hours behind our 959, which occupies the first place in the standings. René Metge knows that this last stage to Dakar is just for show, so he avoids taking unnecessary risks.

Even so, we're going at over 93mph (150km/h), making our mark on the sand next to the sea, getting our tyres wet once in a while and saluting the great ocean that bears witness to this unusual spectacle every year. As we get closer to the end the number of spectators on the beach increases, until we're met by a 'sea' of people at the finish line of this great and hard marathon. Metge slows down as he reaches the finish line and the other two 959s that departed from Paris join us, the no.185 of Ickx/Brasseur and the no.187 of Kussmaul/Unger, which, by finishing in sixth place, contributes decisively to the extraordinary group result of Porsche.

*We cross the finish line, the three cars are immediately surrounded by specta-
tors, journalist and photographers wishing to enjoy and register the moment.
Among them is Peter Falk, our racing director, radiant with yet another success
that clearly shows Porsche's potential, happy and proud with the work done by
the great team behind this feat. Metge and Lemoyne are ecstatic, climbing on
top of the roof of the 959 and tasting the victory champagne!*

*During this time of celebration, I remember some of the most significant
moments during the three weeks of the race that will forever be recorded in the
memory of those involved: the passage through Algeria at a relatively calm pace;
the crossing of the Ténéré Desert, where we drove at above 124mph (200km/h)
over the harder sand and where we took the lead of the race; the increased
navigational difficulties for Lemoyne in the 217.5-mile (350km) night stage from
Iferouane to Agadez; the shock and grief felt by all in the 'bivouac' at Gourma,
after confirmation of the death of Thierry Sabine, the director and great builder
of the Paris–Dakar, plus four other people, in a helicopter accident, when they
were going to the end of the day's stage; the crossing of the north zone of the
Niger river, with the ground alternating from soft sand to tyre-destroying rocks;
the passage through the Bandiagara Escarpment; the 526-mile (847km) special
stage between Bamako and Mamou with parts among 3m-high vegetation; and
at last our arrival at the beaches of Dakar and the view of the Atlantic Ocean.*

**The three
Porsche 959s
enrolled in the
1986 Paris–
Dakar rally at
an intermediate
assistance point
during a typical
African stage.**

René Metge and Dominique Lemoyne in the 959 achieved a fantastic victory in the demanding 1986 Paris–Dakar rally.

This was Porsche's second win in this extraordinary race, since it had already won in 1984, also with Metge and Lemoyne, in a 911 4×4 'prototype', making up for the fact that it had never won the other charismatic road race of the African continent, Kenya's Safari. The name and fame of the Paris–Dakar surpassed even that of the Safari and Porsche took advantage of that fact by demonstrating the endurance and technical advancement of the winning cars.

The victorious 959 in 1986 was in fact a 'showcase' of technology, based on the car introduced at the Frankfurt Automotive Show in 1983, and which Porsche had decided to produce in a limited series of 200 units. It was an almost entirely new car, since it incorporated few components of the 911, thus presenting completely innovative technical solutions: computer-managed all-wheel drive, which allowed for the distribution of power between the rear and forward wheels through a multidisc clutch, making it possible to send up to 50 per cent of the power to the front axle; suspension with double shock absorbers, giving the possibility of varying the distance to the ground; an engine with water-cooled cylinder heads with 4 valves per cylinder, fuelled by twin sequential turbochargers, which put out 450bhp (reduced to 400 for the African race); and Kevlar bodywork components (roof, doors and hoods).

The fact that the 959s not only won this hard race but also managed to finish with the three cars that were enrolled, demonstrated the validity of the technical solutions that were used in these difficult and demanding terrains and also the mechanical endurance needed to vanquish the obstacles along the way. Porsche proved that it could produce excellent cars that allowed it to win automotive competitions as different as the 24 Hours of Le Mans and the Paris–Dakar.

19 SEPTEMBER 1989, ZELL AM SEE, AUSTRIA

Today is a special day at Zell am See, as Ferry Porsche's eightieth birthday is being celebrated and the party prepared in his honour at Schloss Prielau is about to begin. There are many guests attending: family and friends, old and current Porsche collaborators and other individuals connected to the automobile industry and politics. Upon arrival, all the guests have the opportunity to enjoy the impressive 'honour guard' consisting of illustrious cars that proudly carry the Porsche crest. These are some of the most outstanding cars made in Stuttgart-Zuffenhausen, which achieved their laurels on the circuits of the most famous competitions in automotive sport, or simply on the roads and highways of various countries.

Along the wooded walkways you can see: a 936 and a 956 (winners of Le Mans); a 908/3 of the Targa Florio; a 911 of the Paris–Dakar; and many other competition or series production cars, representing the forty-one years of the brand's existence. But among them, right next to the tent where in a short while the ceremony will begin, is a very special Porsche that was built on purpose for this occasion. It is in fact my 'passport' into this special event!

In the first row at Ferry Porsche's side are his daughters-in-law and his sons, Ferdinand Alexander ('Butzi'), Gerhard Anton, Hans-Peter and Wolfgang Heinz. Let us pay attention because the ceremony is about to begin and Wolfgang Porsche starts his welcome speech for all the guests:

I want to welcome you on behalf of myself and my brothers. We are extremely pleased that you have come to Prielau on the occasion of my father's eightieth birthday. Our family feels especially attached to this beautiful countryside and we are naturally very happy that Zell am See greeted our guests with such wonderful weather. The cars that form your guard of honour represent four decades in the history of the still-young Porsche automobile marque, which our father founded in Gmünd and Stuttgart.

But our view today reaches even further back: to the era when our father and grandfather worked together in the Porsche design offices, and to the early years in Wiener Neustadt and Stuttgart. The life of our father, which we are privileged to look back on today, also constitutes a slice of automobile history…

The speeches continue with an attentive crowd. Walther Zügel speaks for the Supervisory Board:

Porsche – the fascination. Porsche – an image in the world which many, even millions, know and admire. Porsche – a vehicle beloved by many, even those who aren't motor racing fans, for its power, its dynamics, the ruggedness of its singing engine. Driving in its finest form, expressing a way of life, as provided by Porsche.

We are all grateful, my dear Professor Porsche, that you will continue to leave your mark on this firm for the foreseeable future, by word and deed, as Supervisory Board Chairman. We learnt as well to comprehend difficult times for what they really are – challenges. Challenges to draw strength for new and fearless accomplishments.

We are thankful for your attention. We wish you my dear Professor Porsche, a long life to come.

Now it is time for Heinz Branitzki, CEO of Porsche AG, to speak:

It is clear to us all that not only the guests gathered here but also a vast community of Porsche drivers, Porsche friends and Porsche admirers worldwide is with you in spirit today, on the occasion of your eightieth birthday. Appreciation of your influence and your merits, not only for the Porsche company but for the automobile itself, is our obligation.

You grew up with the aroma of gasoline, under the direction of your already legendary father, the 'old Professor' as he is known today. At your birth, on 19 September 1909, in Wiener Neustadt, Ferdinand Anton Ernst Porsche, your father, was driving in the Semmering Hill Climb. He won his class, launching a racing tradition.

Sporting success came as early as 1950, achieved by customers, while a works Porsche started at Le Mans in 1951 and immediately won its class. Since that time, it is impossible to imagine not only Le Mans, but race tracks around the world, without Porsche cars.

You have always had an infallible feeling for the fascination of this sport, especially for our customers, going beyond the question of racing enriching production cars. Those who observed you earlier at major foreign events know this. You always spent the 24 Hours of Le Mans with the team. Whereas drivers and helpers receive the finest care today, earlier efforts were primitive and hard as nails. You never failed to sit with your people in the pits for 24 hours of heat, dust, rain or ice-cold nights, always approachable if a problem should arise.

In the name of the entire firm, from the Board, the Workers' Council, down to the least mechanic and those countless Porsche friends around the world, I would like to present our sincere wishes for good luck and good fortune on your eightieth birthday. May God guard and protect you.

Despite his already debilitated health, it is now Ferry Porsche's turn to speak:

Ladies and gentlemen, my dear guests, I want to thank you with all my heart for coming, for your congratulations and for the words of praise. I find it difficult to form the proper words for what I feel today.

I am naturally pleased that so many nice things were said about me. But I want to remind you all that success of Porsche company was only made possible by all those people who stood by my side and devoted their energies to it.

I have tried all my life to be a good man. I want to thank all those who helped me. And I thank all of those from whom I have learned during my life.

But I also want to thank our customers and our dealers, among whose ranks I have found many personal friends. I am pleased that all of you could be with me on this wonderful day and hope you will have a most pleasant time.[35]

The crowd applauds Ferry Porsche, who, being surrounded by friends and family members, is certainly very happy. There are many familiar faces: his sister Louise Piech with her son Ferdinand Piech, Huschke von Hanstein, Hans Herrmann, Helmuth Bott and many other relevant figures in the brand's history. But now comes a very special moment, the delivery of Ferry Porsche's birthday gift. Special for him without a doubt, but also special for me since I'm living it too! The cover that 'wraps' the present is removed and an admiration-filled gasp is heard

Ferry Porsche with his sons (from left) Hans-Peter, Gerhard, Ferdinand Alexander and Wolfgang on his eightieth birthday at Schloss Prielau near Zell am See. The Panamericana was his very special birthday present.

among the guests. In front of everyone is the Porsche Panamericana, a one of a kind, made specifically for this moment. A unique present for a unique moment!

Ferry Porsche and many of the guests attending admire the boldness of the car's lines. It shines in a single colour, a special green that contrasts well with its interior and its top, which can be removed using a zipper, making the original car into a cabriolet. Ferry Porsche and all his sons are now around the Panamericana, with the photographers registering this outstanding moment. It was well worth it to 'get into' this project to see its development and this unique moment!

The Panamericana was developed in a short six-month period by the design department under the guidance of Harm Lagaay. It was a concept car based upon the mechanics of the 964. Unseen was its roof, which could be disassembled, as well as the rear window that could be easily removed by opening a zipper. Another peculiarity was that due to the unique design of the wheel arches, it could use different types and sizes of rims and tyres, which could be adjusted to different uses. The possibility of the concept car originating a series model was considered, but would be abandoned. However, its lines ended up influencing aspects of the 993 and the Boxster, which was perhaps to be expected since the responsibility for the design of these models also belonged to Harm Lagaay.

Currently the Panamericana can be enjoyed at the Porsche Museum, where some of its details, like the aforementioned zipper and the design of its tyres' tread with the Porsche symbol, continue to impress the most observant visitors.

CHAPTER SIX

PORSCHE: MORE THAN JUST CARS

14–17 AUGUST 1998, LAGUNA SECA, USA

The Laguna Seca circuit is once again filled with enthusiasts of automotive sport for the Monterey Historics event that is held here every year. But this edition has a very special point of interest, since Porsche has decided to celebrate its fifty years as an automobile marque by bringing twenty cars from its museum, which, together with others coming from different places, will delight the many visitors, among whom a clear predominance of the brand's fans can be witnessed.

For many of the American fans, this will be a unique opportunity to see together some of the most charismatic Porsches, where the following stand out: the 356/1, the distinguished 'grandfather' of all the others[36]; the 356 SL of the 1951 24 Hours of Le Mans; the 550 no.55 of the Carrera Panamericana of 1954; a 718 F2; several 718s, 904s, 906s, 910s, 907s, 908s, 917s and the powerful 917/10

At the 1998 Monterey Historics in Laguna Seca Porsche celebrated its fiftieth birthday as a car manufacturer, gathering the most extensive line-up of Porsche race cars ever.

and 917/30 winners of the Can-Am; several 911s in its multiple variants, with the no.14 of the East African Safari of 1978 and the 959 of the 1986 Paris–Dakar standing out; several 956s and 962s; the 936s that won Le Mans in 1976, 1977 and 1981, and many others. It is an incredible feast for the eyes of the many enthusiasts in attendance.

For me, this is a very special moment, because after almost ten years of 'sleeping' at the museum in Zuffenhausen, finally the opportunity arose to come back to a more active and challenging life, since I caught a ride in the 550 no.55 of the Carrera Panamericana directly to the other side of the Atlantic!

The rest of the weekend is a fantastic revival of good feelings, both on the track, where there are lively races (Hans Herrmann is still in great shape!) and in the pits where, in a quieter environment, it is great to see again other charismatic personalities of the brand: Derek Bell, George Follmer, Herbert Linge, Hurley Haywood, Walter Röhrl and others. Wolfgang Porsche is also in attendance, making this important moment shine even more. It culminates with an impressive family photo, in which there are more than seventy Porsches (surely as 'proud' as their owners!), representing fifty years of success and the realization of the dreams of its founders.

There is no doubt that this attitude of Porsche to attend regularly these significant events and satisfy the desires of aficionados is a trait that distinguishes it from the competition, making us all feel like part of a great 'family', which likes to get together to enjoy unique moments and the pleasure of being a 'Porschist'.

From the more modest regional Porsche Club meetings to the great annual meetings like the Porsche Parade in the USA (where there are always more than 1,000 cars and 2,000 enthusiasts), the spirit is the same, to enjoy the pleasure of owning and driving a Porsche, to spend time and share experiences with others and to admire the beauty of the different cars, that sometimes are driven hundreds or even thousands of kilometres to attend.

AUGUST 2000, NEVADA DESERT, USA

A few minutes after 05:00 the sun rises over the Nevada Desert, turning the barren ground a shade of reddish brown that contrasts with the black asphalt line crossing it. The scene would be absolutely calm if it wasn't for the bustling filming team that surrounds us. I'm anxious for the action to begin, after a 2-hour trip locked in the back of a truck, because what is to come will surely be worth remembering.

Porsche has brought its most recent and secret 'weapon', still unknown to the general public, to this remote landscape for the creation of a presentation film. Everything has been planned to the smallest detail, from the location to the technical and logistical support that is necessary. The car already has a name – the Carrera GT, a name that demands by itself a machine that lives up to the history of the brand. Shining in its Silver Argent paint, the car now reflects the first rays of sunlight, adding a different chromatic tone that contrasts perfectly with the scenery around us.

Walter Röhrl drives the Carrera GT in the Nevada Desert.

The Carrera GT is a showcase of technology, from the chassis and body-work panels in carbon, to the engine, a powerful and light V10 with 560bhp. Fortunately for me, aluminium is still part of the solution, both structurally (central tunnel and door reinforcements) and aesthetically in the cockpit where it is 'brushed', giving a special touch of design to the interior that is also innovative.

Walter Röhrl has just sat down and is enjoying the interior, which is not only beautiful but also functional. You can see a smile on his face when his hand rests on the gear shifter, which is positioned almost at steering wheel height, as he feels the 'warm' touch of the birch and ash with which the sphere on top of the lever is made. This interesting nod to the competition prototypes introduces not only another detail of fine taste and respect for the maxim of 'form follows function', but also hints at an obligation to the car's illustrious ancestors.

Now is the moment that I've been longing for, to wake up the V10 that responds to the first press on the starter button. A harmonious sound that announces respectable power is released from the two exhausts and turns the heads of all the people around us that are waiting for the magic word – 'Action'. Having received the signal from the director of filming, Walter Röhrl starts off following the Jeep that is carrying on its open back the equipment and personnel necessary to capture the first images.

The 'secret' Carrera GT presentation film occupied a dedicated Walter Röhrl during five days on Nevada Desert roads.

The speed increases as the black asphalt, where the two yellow lines stand out, falls away under our car, which seems almost to levitate! I can see the astonished looks on the faces of the people in the Jeep in front of us, who are surely getting wonderful images, now that behind us a cloud formation reflects the reddish tones of the sun and the desert, giving our morning ride even more of a 'space voyage' look.

The Carrera GT was undoubtedly the new Porsche flagship at the beginning of the twenty-first century.

And what a ride it is, the pleasure of rolling in this supercar, in such special scenery, enjoying both its technical attributes and the nature that surrounds us. One can only remember Ferry Porsche's words: 'Driving in its finest form!'

Five days of filming, in which the team got up at 03:00, were necessary to ensure that there would be enough raw footage. Besides the technical aspects, the team had to take special care to keep the operation away from curious eyes. Filming was interrupted several times whenever the alert was given by strategically placed observers that a car was approaching. Walter Röhrl would bring the Carrera GT quickly back to base and it was promptly covered and the action was only restarted when the scene was clear again.

This behaviour was fundamental to ensuring that the presentation of the car at the Paris Auto Show at the end of September would be a complete surprise to all the public, including the most news-digging reporters. And so it was, but Porsche had another surprise for the media. Having not only revealed its new car in the show itself, as is tradition, Porsche also sent a press release to the different news agencies, summoning them to be present at 06:00 on 28 September next to the Louvre Pyramid.

Without knowing what to expect, over 400 journalists accepted the challenge and after a few minutes they had the privilege of hearing a special 'growl' coming from a car that was approaching, illuminating the Louvre Pyramid and the people around it with its powerful xenon headlights. After a first instant of bewilderment, the flashes started firing at an unstoppable rhythm and the looks of surprise and astonishment were the most common among those attending, confirming the first impressions gained from a viewing of the Nevada Desert film, which they had been invited to see minutes before in an amphitheatre inside the museum.

Walter Röhrl was once again the driver of the Carrera GT. The day had started at 03:00, next to the Arc de Triomphe, where the new Porsche flagship had come down from a truck. The rain was present as a small setback, but it did not wilt the team's spirit as they accompanied Röhrl along the Champs-Élysées, the Place de la Concorde and finally the Louvre.

Walter Röhrl starts his night ride in Paris from the Arc de Triomphe to the Louvre Pyramid, where the new Carrera GT will be presented to journalists and reporters, before its exhibition at the Paris Auto Show.

That was how, with this well-prepared and unusual media spectacle, Paris and the automotive world came to know the car that would be considered the great event of the Auto Show and the paradigm of the early twenty-first century sports car. The audience was unanimous in considering the Carrera GT an exceptional car and it was admired for its design, technical characteristics and the quality of its make. Details of the engine, such as the beautiful intake manifolds, which stood out through a thin metal mesh that accompanied the shape of the hood, emphasized even more the care and inspiration of the design office. With the open hood, the push-rod suspension elements and the quality of the entire build, one is reminded a high-quality Swiss watch.

A car like this can inevitably cause those who admire it to dream and even more so when one makes note of the announced performance: 205mph (330km/h) and less than 4 seconds from 0–60mph (0–100km/h). After the final developments of the project, the first units, almost exactly like the car presented in Paris, started coming out of the new factory at Leipzig and were delivered to their fortunate owners in 2003, eighteen years after the technological showcase of that other Porsche landmark, the 959.

15 MARCH 2008, SEBRING, USA

After a long break during which I couldn't enjoy the thrill of racing, I have finally managed to get back into action. Since 2006, I have been looking for an opportunity to 'try out' the machine that Porsche has built to get back officially into competition, the RS Spyder. Due to an adverse set of circumstances, I have had to wait for the beginning of the 2008 season, but I have now seized my chance and am here at the start of the 12 Hours of Sebring.

It's now 10:00 on this Saturday morning and the beautiful yellow RS Spyder no.6 is on the starting grid, having obtained the best time for the LMP2 (Le Mans Prototype) cars, but behind the more powerful LMP1s, the Peugeot 908 and Audi R10, which occupy the first rows. Of course, theoretically the LMP1s will always be the favourites to win, but the Porsche is betting on its lower weight and greater agility to bring the fight to the 'big boys'.

In fact, this year's RS Spyder is a more powerful evolution (503bhp), but it is also slightly heavier (weighing 1,821lb/826kg) than the car that ran in 2007, due to changes in the regulations. To the surprise of many, last year's car had been able to beat the LMP1 cars in several races of the Championship. Romain Dumas, Timo Bernhard and Emmanuel Collard, who are driving the no.7 car, are going to give it their best, as well as their colleagues Patrick Long, Sascha Maassen and Ryan Briscoe in the no.6 RS Spyder, to beat the Audis and Peugeots.

Romain Dumas is now watching the cars in front and as soon as the pace car leaves the track he steps on the accelerator and here we go at great speed towards the first corner. The engine has a very pleasant sound and the car accelerates vigorously, but we can't keep up with the LMP1 cars that take the lead with the Peugeot 908 in front of the two Audi R10s. In these first laps we're in a direct fight within the LMP2 class with the Acuras and also with the RS Spyder enrolled by the Dyson private team. Within half an hour of racing, the first yellow flags come out when the Audi no.1 of Rinaldo Capello rams the Porsche GT3 RSR of Johannes van Overbeek, causing the cars of the different classes to group up behind the leader, the Peugeot 908 of Nicolas Minassian.

The usual adventures of a 12-hour race occur, allowing for successive changes in the lead, but with the Peugeot and the Audis initially prevailing in the fight for first position. However, the Peugeot is forced to retire even before the halfway point with problems in the gearbox's hydraulic command and the no.2 Audi has problems with its turbo, making it unable to continue to fight for the win. The other RS Spyder of the Roger Penske team is not in the running either, as it has

Porsche wins the 2008 12 Hours of Sebring with the RS Spyder of Romain Dumas, Timo Bernhard and Emmanuel Collard.

had to retire with engine problems. The no.1 Audi that has led for many laps is now stopped in the pits with some sort of problem that the mechanics are trying to solve.

We are going into the last hour of the race and it is the RS Spyder no.20 of the Dyson team that is leading, with us in second place. Romain Dumas is giving it all he's got and lap after lap is reducing the time difference to the leader. His desire to win is enormous, but he also has to defend himself against Adrián Fernández's Acura and Capello's Audi, which is now the fastest on the track after having cured its previous problem and he's gaining quite a lot of time on the others. But Dumas is driving wonderfully and he's thrilled when we overtake the Dyson team car and we take the lead!

The win is close and it is with relief that at the end of 12 hours of extraordinary racing we see the chequered flag. Porsche wins again at the 12 Hours of Sebring, twenty years after its last win in this famous race!

Effectively, this was Porsche's first win in a renowned race after its official comeback to competition in 2005. After the decision made in 1998 by Porsche's directors to invest in the development of a new range of models rather than racing, it was necessary to start almost from scratch for this comeback, even though it was decided to make a car not for the main class but for the LMP2[37] class.

For the first time, Porsche developed a chassis totally in carbon and employed a new 90-degree V8 engine with 3.4-litres and an initial power of 480bhp. The RS Spyder was mainly aimed at the American competitions integrated in the ALMS[38] Championship, which was run with regulations created by the ACO and which were almost identical to the ones in place at the 24 Hours of Le Mans. The decision to take part in this championship, with races mostly in the United States, took into account the advantage of being able to have the cars run under the Roger Penske team, with which Porsche had always had an excellent relationship.

The RS Spyder took part in the last race in 2005 to test the car, winning its class. In 2006, it participated in the seven races of the Championship, winning the first race in Mid Ohio, beating for the first time the Audi R8s of the LMP1 class and winning the LMP2 class in all the other races. 2007 was an even more spectacular year, since the RS Spyder beat the LMP1 cars in eight of the twelve races of the Championship, winning its class in the other four. But even though 2008 started with the victory at Sebring, it only brought one other overall win, in Utah, but the Dutch team van Merksteijn Motorsport gave joy to Porsche's fans with an LMP2 class win at the 24 Hours of Le Mans. In 2009, Porsche did not run officially with the RS Spyder, but even so it won its class again at Le Mans in the hands of Team Essex.

27 JUNE 2010, PIKES PEAK, USA

Jeff Zwart, behind the wheel of the 911 GT3 Cup, anxiously awaits the starting signal for one of the oldest and most challenging races on the planet, the Pikes Peak Hill Climb, which has run since 1916. It is made up of 12.42 miles (19.99km) and 156 turns to go through as quickly as possible up to the top of the mountain, 4,725ft (1,440m) above the start, where you reach an altitude of 14,115ft (4,300m).

The starter waves the two green flags and Jeff Zwart sets the GT3 free and it quickly gains speed. The sound of the flat-6 invades the cabin, alternating with the characteristic sound of the sequential gearbox that quickly gets to fourth gear before the third turn of the track. In this first part, the surface is asphalt and Zwart is fighting with the steering wheel as the tyres heat up. He goes down into third gear, which he maintains throughout a series of fast turns. These have

Jeff Zwart attacks the 2010 Pikes Peak Hill Climb in the 911 GT3 Cup.

lots of trees on their sides, which are a good indication of the direction of the approaching bends.

In the distance we can see the mountain's peak with some snow remaining along the cliffs. There is now a tight left turn that is done in second gear and right after that Zwart goes quickly through the gears to fifth in a fast but short section, then the car shakes again with successive downshifts until a left hairpin bend, with a steep incline that is done in first gear. At the exit, a new acceleration makes the rear of the 911 skid out of line, a movement that is quickly corrected by Zwart, turning the steering wheel with skill and confidence. And it's only been 2 minutes since the start!

The fun is continuing, since as we climb the difficulties increase. The asphalt starts to be covered with dirt, a sign that we're getting closer to the zone that is not asphalted. We reach this after a hairpin bend done in first gear and now we must be more careful while accelerating at the exit of the turns. Even so, the rear of the GT3 is 'dancing' a bit, although always within limits and without making us lose much time. Next come a series of turns done in second gear and it is a delight to see the ease with which Zwart controls the Porsche and the road. The many spectators on the side of the track are also enjoying the show and they applaud, egging on the veteran driver.

Further ahead, it is noticeable that the trees become fewer, while the cliffs on the sides of the road become more evident and steep. Despite this, there are other very fast areas taken in fourth and fifth gears, alternating with slower turns. Zwart is working hard, but the run remains error-free. We are now about halfway through the climb and the surface turns back into asphalt. We go by a characteristic point with a little guard house in the middle of the road to which we must pay attention, but it is quickly behind us.

After a short straight there is another slower zone with turns in first and second gears, then all of a sudden it seems we're climbing into the sky! The trees are gone, the incline is huge and you can only see road and blue sky in front of us. It is a unique and amazing feeling.

The altitude can be felt, but even with the expected loss of power the engine continues to propel us forward with a speed that is almost reckless, given the

Pikes Peak with Jeff Zwart in a 911 GT3 – a race to the clouds!

terrain. Every once in a while, on the edge of some of the cliffs, there are a few dozen metres of metal guard rails or hay bales, so as to remind us not to overshoot the road. But Zwart is not impressed and continues unshaken, taking the GT3 up the mountain at an impressive pace The spectators are now few and far between and they are replaced on the cliffs by chunks of snow, which soften the roughness of the rocks that dominate the scenery.

The climb to the clouds seems to be without end! Will we take off and continue in a calm and gracious flight? No, the 911 continues firmly 'glued' to the road, even when the most difficult and dangerous part of the climb arrives, again on dirt with fast and hard turns among breathtaking cliffs. We're back in an asphalt zone, signalling that we are now close to the end, about to reach our goal.

After a series of challenging turns there is the last one, a blind left turn that at its end presents us with a vigorous wave of a double chequered flag, with which the race marshal greets all the heroes of the day. Zwart sighs with relief and relaxes while he stops the car in the improvised parking at the peak of such an amazing mountain. These were 11min 31.1sec of pure suspense, adrenalin and pleasure. Thank you, Jeff Zwart, King of the Mountain!

Jeff Zwart is passionate about the Pikes Peak Hill Climb. His participation in 2010 was the ninth since he decided to accept the challenge for the first time in 1994, at the wheel of a Porsche 964 RSR. The Pikes Peak Hill Climb is also known as the 'Race to the Clouds' and holds a particular fascination for many drivers, who come back year after year. Zwart is not a professional driver – he makes his living as a photographer and his work in the automotive industry is well known. This way, he brings together his passion for cars in general, but with a special affection for the Stuttgart brand. The first car he drove was his father's 911 and the first car he bought when he left college was a 914/6, which he still owns today. In 2010, with the time of 11min 31.1sec, he won the 'time attack' 2WD class, even beating the best 4WD car.

Jeff Zwart had always attacked the mountain with series production Porsches with some alterations to make them faster along the 12.42 miles (20km) of the climb. But in 2010 he decided to make a bigger gamble and used for the first time a Porsche made for competition that he had in his garage, a 911 GT3 Cup of 2007. He presented his project to the PMNA,[39] which decided to sponsor the challenge and thus the GT3 was updated with the latest developments, namely a 3.8-litre engine, instead of the original 3.6-litre one.

PMNA also made available a technician to optimize the electronic management of the engine, so that it would work better with the particular conditions at altitude. However, the conditions for testing at Pikes Peak are not the best. The drivers can only test the cars in the practice sessions in the days before the race, but these are done at dawn on three consecutive days, doing a third of the route at a time, since the road cannot be closed to regular traffic during the day. Because of this, the practice conditions are generally different to the ones on the day of the race, a Sunday, namely temperature and humidity, factors that may be influential on the performance of the cars. Furthermore, in the race there is only one climb, one chance, and any error or significant misfortune may mean coming back the following year to try again.

The other extremely important factor is the tyres that are used, since it is all about finding the most balanced solution to deal with both the asphalt and dirt sections of the route. Zwart opted for an unusual and perhaps risky solution, wet tyres supplied by Pirelli. This way, he expected to have a soft tyre, but one that would ensure a 'smooth' transition between the two types of surface. Maybe because of that choice he opted to be one of the first to run on Sunday morning, so that he could avoid higher temperatures.

In the end, his gamble paid off, allowing him to win his class while beating the previous record by 38 seconds. He finished in sixth place in the overall standings, but he was only beaten by cars from the 'Unlimited' and 'Open Wheel' classes, which are built specially for this type of event. At the end of the race, Zwart was extremely happy with his performance and result and was already thinking of the following year's challenge!

Indeed, 2011 was another special year for Jeff Zwart at Pikes Peak, since he took a completely different approach. The car would this time be strictly a series one, the most powerful of all from the Porsche catalogue – the GT2 RS, with 620bhp. To 'spice up' the challenge even more he decided to make the 1,094 miles (1,760km) trip from his home in California to Pikes Peak with the car that he would use to compete! And once again his performance was spectacular, getting a time of 11min 7.8sec, beating his 2010 time by 24 seconds, which is remarkable for a series production car, and getting second place in the 'Time Attack' 2WD class, just behind his great friend Rod Millen, who was 2.9sec faster. At any rate, the GT2 became the fastest street-legal car ever at Pikes Peak. At the end of the event, the incredible Jeff Zwart said: 'I have 364 days to think about next year's race!' Remarkable for a fifty-six year-old youngster!

Jeff Zwart at the 2011 Pikes Peak with the 911 GT2 RS he drove from California to Colorado.

In fact, Zwart did not return in 2012, but he did in 2013 with yet another totally different project that gathered the best of two worlds: the chassis of the 2010 GT3 Cup combined with the power of the 2011 GT2 RS turbo engine. Despite this explosive mix, he did not win the 'Time Attack' class but came in second, beating his 2011 time by over 1 minute, totalling 10min 13.85sec. This was also partly due to the fact that the entire route was now covered in asphalt, allowing for the use of slick tyres.

For 2014, Zwart decided to continue with the same car, with some small improvements, including new gearbox ratios. But during the race there were problems with the fuel pump that did not allow him to fight for the win, although even so his time improved again, with the climb completed in 10min 1.9sec. Without those problems, Zwart would no doubt have entered the elite club of those who have climbed Pikes Peak in under 10 minutes.

Jeff Zwart goes up the mountain at an impressive pace.

In 2015, with his very special GT3 turbo, Jeff Zwart entered the elite club of those who have climbed Pikes Peak in less than 10 minutes.

That was the challenge for 2015, which was conquered, since the GT3 Cup, equipped with an even more powerful turbo engine (over 700bhp), completed the extraordinary climb with a magnificent time of 9min 46.24sec, winning the class and definitively entering Zwart into the Kings of the Mountain club!

I don't know if Jeff Zwart will participate for a fifteenth time in this mythical race. His fourteen participations in ten different Porsches are already a remarkable epic tale. His heart and the will to best himself are huge, but at 61 years of age he is entitled to think twice about going up a mountain road with cliffs by its side at speeds over 124mph (200km/h)!

In any case it was Jeff Zwart himself that said 'This mountain has a special magic that keeps you coming back.'

5–10 APRIL 2011, TASMANIA

The 911 SC that the Porsche Museum has brought to the other side of the world is about to begin one of the most charismatic classic car races of the southern hemisphere, the twentieth running of the Targa Tasmania. The white 911 with red stripes is part of a group of four cars that Klaus Bischoff has brought to this faraway place for the enjoyment of the Australian fans.

As they sit in the car, Walter Röhrl and his navigator Christian Geistdörfer recall the adventures they lived through in the San Remo Rally thirty years earlier, in which they fought for the win almost until the end, when a drive shaft unfortunately broke. Three decades later and with the car's recent restoration carried out by the technicians at the museum in Zuffenhausen the team is together again, this time for more casual and fun-filled roles. But Röhrl, besides wanting to have fun, never fully leaves behind his competitive side.

Walter Röhrl is always ready to give his best, even in a classic car event like the 2011 Targa Tasmania, where he pushes forward with the 911 SC.

The Tasmanian roads suit well the 911 SC's agility and Walter Röhrl's driving skills.

However, Röhrl knows that the power the 911 has available (250bhp) is not enough to oppose others that are more powerful and he will only have a chance if the weather conditions help him, namely with rain, lots of rain! But his request is unanswered and there is a radiant sun out when Röhrl, after putting his helmet on, starts off for the first leg of the rally. The race will play out for five days and 1,243 miles (2,000km), with forty special stages that Geistdörfer will have to guide him through.

Despite the efforts of Röhrl, with the dry weather and on these very good asphalt roads, it is unavoidable to lose 1 or 2 seconds per kilometre to the fastest cars. It's now almost noon on the second stage when, during a connection route between timed stages, a loud noise comes from the back on the left side and forces Röhrl to stop. He steps out of the car and can't really believe it when he realizes that a drive shaft has broken, just like thirty years ago on an Italian road! A bit disappointed, he tells Geistdorfer that everything is over and that they can start thinking about the return flight. But Geistdorfer knows W. Rohrl well enough to foresee that it won't really be like that! After a temporary fix, we manage to conclude the stage, but we are now in 95th position among 103 contestants. While the 911 is being repaired, I wonder whether this adventure will still continue the next morning, but Röhrl shows up in the parc fermé with his racing suit on and helmet in his hand – the fun will continue! The third leg plays out with Röhrl in a good mood (despite the sun) and he keeps getting consecutive second and third places in the special stages.

We get to the fourth day and almost at the end of the leg the rain finally makes an appearance! Röhrl rejoices and in the 11 miles (18km) of this qualifying stage we gain 30 seconds on the leader, which is also a Porsche (Carrera RS with 320bhp). The following special stage with 20.75 miles (33.4km) is done in really adverse conditions for most of the teams, with heavy rain, almost no visibility and mud and gravel on the road surface. But Röhrl is in his environment and he gets another 30 seconds back, to the amazement of his adversaries!

After recovering many places in the standings and a good night's rest, the fifth leg is about to begin, still with a lot of rain. Röhrl presses hard and he makes yet more gains in the slippery stages. We complete the longest stage of the race, 36.7 miles (59km), with the amazing average of 74.5mph (120km/h). Arriving in

Walter Röhrl and Christian Geistdörfer, despite an early mechanical problem, managed to finish the Targa Tasmania in tenth place, attacking hard in the last stages.

Hobart at the end of this five-day odyssey, Röhrl's effort is rewarded with tenth place in the final standings, after a spectacular recovery. When he is interviewed about his performance, he lets out: 'If only there had been more rain!'

Participation in classic car events plays an important role in the Porsche Museum's annual activities and is without doubt a manifestation of its respect and care for all those who, throughout the years, have driven, maintained and applauded the brand's cars in races held in all continents.

15–17 JULY 2011, CIRCUIT DE LA SARTHE, LE MANS, FRANCE

There is a great bustle in the paddock at the de la Sarthe circuit. The mechanics have just unloaded the last cars that came from the museum in four transport trucks. For three days, French aficionados and others will be able to enjoy fine moments, as Porsche is celebrating two historic events at this festival: fifty years of Porsche Clubs in France and thirty years since the launch of the 944.

It is a very special 944 that brought me here from the museum. In fact, it is not really a 944, but officially a 924 GTP Le Mans, which participated in the 24 Hours here in 1981, finishing in an honourable seventh place in the general standing and driven by Walter Röhrl and Jürgen Barth. It may be considered as a prototype (even though it is quite a bit more 'muscular') of the 944 that would be commercialized soon. Porsche wanted in this way to pay homage to the thirty years of the model, sending a special ambassador with its own history at the French circuit.

I'm now behind the stands of the circuit's pits, under a tent raised to protect the cars and receive visitors. I am without a doubt in good company, as also here with me on my right is the 911 no.76 of the 1984 Paris–Dakar and the 935 'baby' no.40; to my left is a 911 RSR turbo from the 1974 Le Mans, a beautiful 930 and a magnificent 356 Carrera Abarth. Engineer Alexander Klein is organizing the

The Porsche
Museum
brought some
representative
cars of the
marque's
history to the
2011 Porsche
Festival held
at the Le Mans
circuit.

display of the cars and ensuring that everything is in order for when the event is opened to the public on the following morning.

And when the doors open at 09:00, despite the threatening sky that's looking like rain, the festival goers start to arrive and are parking their Porsches in the parks reserved for them, which continue to fill up during the day in a very colourful way. These fans are fantastic and attend these events unconditionally, thus justifying that they take place. But the fans won't just enjoy the Porsches on display, since nearly all of them, even the ones that came from the museum, will go out on track, naturally not using the normal 24-hour race circuit, but rather the Bugatti circuit, which shares the start/finish straight and the route until the Esses after the Dunlop curve.

The mechanics have raised the bonnet lid of the 924 GTP and started the engine, so that it can heat up a bit before going out on the track. With each press of the accelerator the engine 'roars', although still with an irregular sound and some back-firing. After a few minutes the lid is put back down and Romain Dumas sits behind the wheel. He fastens his seat belt, does some more quick revs, then drives calmly towards the gate to access the track.

We are at the end of the pit lane and Dumas accelerates towards the Dunlop curve, calmly checking that everything is working correctly and carefully increasing the speed because it is the first time that he has driven the 924. I'm enjoying every moment. How good it is to be here and running around this special track again, even if it is at a somewhat leisurely pace. Following the pace car (a Cayenne) are the museum's cars, the 935 driven by Gérard Larrousse, the 911 4x4 driven by René Metge and behind them a series of Porsche 924s, 944s and 968s belonging to the French club,[40] which is one of the main organizers of the event.

How these fans must be happy to drive around with such illustrious company! After them come the Porsches of the most diverse models and years, which belong to other fans attending the event and who do not miss out on the chance to bring their cars on to the track. It is their party and will continue to be so for three days, with several parades, as well as some races that will thrill drivers and spectators.

Everything will come to a close on Sunday with the Grand Parade that will bring on to the track almost all the festival goers and their cars for some unforgettable laps. Meanwhile, between the parades and the races, the cars return to the paddock where the visitors are growing in number. It is fantastic to see how they enjoy these machines and how much they know about their characteristics and history. I notice now one of those fans beside me talking with Alexander Klein and telling him that he drove 1,000 miles (1,600km) in his 944 S2 to be here! He is not a young man, his grey beard indicating a respectable age, but his enthusiasm is enormous as he enjoys the environment and company and being able to see and even touch the cars that have fuelled his passion for many years.

And all of a sudden I have an idea … why not try to 'live' some time with an anonymous Porsche enthusiast? Okay, it is decided and if destiny wills it, it will be so! Meanwhile, Dumas, still sitting at the wheel of the 924 GTP, talks with Klein, while some tables and chairs are being prepared for an autograph session with

The 924 GTP was one of the stars of the festival. This car, driven by Jürgen Barth and Walter Röhrl, had achieved seventh place overall in the 1981 24 Hours of Le Mans and it was a prototype of the future 944, whose thirtieth birthday was celebrated at the event.

Dumas, Larrousse and Metge. And now Dumas asks Klein a question about the gearbox, while he touches the gear lever… Bingo! The first step of the 'migration' process is complete. Dumas in now sitting in his chair next to Metge, to start giving out the posters that are on the table. These are quite beautiful posters, representing all the Porsche victories in the 24 Hours of Le Mans and Dumas is certainly wishing to become part of this 'club' in the not so distant future.

The Porsche fans follow one another. Some exchange some brief words with the drivers and I see that the next one in line is that enthusiast who was speak-

The Porsche fans could take a close look at the cars and get information from drivers and mechanics.

The decoration of this GT3 Cup recalls Porsche's first-class victory in the 1951 24 Hours of Le Mans.

Romain Dumas autographs posters commemo- rating the sixteen Porsche victories at the 24 Hours of Le Mans.

ing earlier with Klein. It's him I'm putting my money on! Dumas asks his name, signs the poster and they talk for a bit. Dumas is also surprised by the long trip he took to be here and finally the fan thanks him and extends his hand for a handshake … bingo again! It's done! I've just stepped on to an unknown and different stage.

While I don't immediately come into contact with the fan's car, which will be my new 'home' for a while, I enjoy the rest of the day 'accompanying' its owner on his walkabout through the paddock. There is much to enjoy here: a 'small' 910 whose engine a mechanic has just started, with its sound arousing the

A well- preserved and nimble 910 goes to the track.

attention of many enthusiasts who quickly surround it; further ahead a beautiful 962 that the mechanics are pushing; and now right in front of us is a fantastic 917 in the traditional GULF colours, which leaves the paddock towards the race track with its unique sound that many follow in admiration.

The hours go by rapidly and I can sense the growing satisfaction of the Porsche fan I'm 'accompanying'. That satisfaction hits its peak when he sits in the passen- ger seat of a 911 GT3 Cup for several laps around the circuit at the side of Vincent Capillaire, a driver and instructor at the circuit. These laps provide an unforget- table experience for the fan and others who have signed up for it. They fully appreciate Porsche making this 'adventure' available to them. The wide smile at the end of the experience is a good indication of the thrilling moments the

It is always 'magic' to see and hear a 917 speeding up at the start/finish straight of the Le Mans circuit.

fan has just experienced. But the best is yet to come, when in the evening the organization announces that the reception dinner for the many fans attending will be held outdoors, with the tables set up along the start/finish straight of the Le Mans circuit! This is something that has never been done before, truly symbolic and probably unrepeatable!'

At the end of the unforgettable dinner, it was time to come into contact with the 944 S2, when the fans started to head to their respective cars in the parking lots. I realize then that the car in which I hope to enjoy some different and interesting moments is a beautiful white cabriolet, which is over twenty years old but is well taken care of and welcoming.

A 911 GT3 RS 4.0 on the start/finish straight delights the festival goers that are going to take their places at the tables behind for the unforgettable and unique reception dinner.

The climax of the festival is the Sunday parade, in which more than 400 cars are taking part. The coming together of Porsches of all ages and models is a remarkable sight. We're now lined up in front of the pits, three per row, and after a few minutes of waiting until everything is ready, we head out on to the track behind the museum's and the 924-944-968 Club's cars, a seemingly endless line of Porsches. We approach the Dunlop Bridge with a beautiful yellow 996 GT3 to our left, then at the Esses take the right turn into the Bugatti circuit and along its short straights and turns the spectacle is impressive. The cars fill the entire circuit, we're driving almost at walking pace, but we don't care about speed right now, just being together.

And what a great pleasure it is to arrive at the entrance to the start/finish straight and recognize the familiar scenery (but experiencing it as if it were the first time) – the control tower on the right, the stands on the left, the Dunlop turn in the distance. On the straight the drivers can accelerate a bit more, freeing the 'horses' under the hood, and what a pleasure it is to feel the acceleration and speed and realize that we are on 'sacred ground' where so many glorious victories have been achieved!

After the magnificent parade, it is already the afternoon and the fans start to depart. It is time for goodbyes but we have stayed almost until closing time, wanting to prolong as much as possible the extraordinary moments we experienced here. There is a slight drizzle and only half a dozen cars in our park, when we set off and leave the circuit. See you next time! And now it seems I have a

Hundreds of Porsches get ready to enter the Le Mans track for the Sunday final parade.

1,000-mile (1,600km) trip in front of me to the garage that will host me for the near future.

This Porsche festival has been an outstanding and unforgettable event. It was a dream come true, made very special by some pleasant surprises, making me understand even better what the Porsche 'family' is and how it is enriched by events like these. It has made me feel 'younger' and with the (somewhat strange) feeling of having my 'Porschist spirit' reinforced!

AUGUST 2011/APRIL 2012, PORTUGAL

Members of Porsche Club Portugal enjoy the beautiful landscape during a meeting organized by the club at Arouca in the north of the country.

With the decision I have taken to spend some time with a Porsche fan, I now understand much better the passion of a fan for the marque. Besides the special care he takes with his car, I can feel his thrill every time he opens the garage door and sees his car ready for another drive. Even if it is just a short one, the experience always feels new and invigorating, as he relaxes calmly while driving on a nearly deserted road by the sea, with the top down and leaving any troubles behind. Or he may be planning for the next club meeting where he will get together with other enthusiasts. Here he will share their company and their experiences in their cars, travelling in a convoy on the way to find new roads and landscapes. Sometimes they are invited by the Porsche dealership for a presentation of a new model. Or I can feel his joy just sitting in a café, enjoying a drink and gazing adoringly at his Porsche. He may even whisper to his car, confiding a doubt he may have, or a new source of joy, or asking for help in a tough decision. He feels a great thrill when he sees the brand winning a major automotive

competition, or when he reads magazines and books, sees films about its history, or when he visits the museum and comes into direct contact with that history.

I realized during these months that the pleasures and the rewards for a Porsche enthusiast can be of many different kinds. Each one of them will certainly give more value to some than to others, but the feeling of belonging to a great family that is cherished by the brand itself is without a doubt common to most of them.

At the beginning of 2012, my 'host' is particularly enthused about the possibility of going to Stuttgart in May for the big commemoration of the sixty years of Porsche Clubs. And it is with happiness that I see him rejoice when he receives the confirmation of his participation in the event. It will also provide a chance to return to my origins, after having passed these last months in a different way, coming to understand one of the reasons behind the secret of Porsche's success – the passion and fascination of its clients for the cars, as well as for the brand and its history.

25–27 MAY 2012, ZUFFENHAUSEN, GERMANY

How pleasant it is to be at the Porsche Platz in Zuffenhausen again, standing before the magnificent museum and the factory buildings, from which cars have been leaving for more than sixty years, to the great satisfaction of clients and fans alike. We are immediately impressed by the sight of a fine 356 A parked by the entrance, still with its identification plates from the historic Mille Miglia, from where it has returned just a few days ago. But we will have to wait for the

The Porsche Museum impresses everyone with its spectacular architecture.

A pristine Porsche 356, recently returned from the Mille Miglia historic rally, is exhibited in front of the museum main entrance.

next day to enter the museum, since it's almost 18:00 and the museum is about to close its doors.

After a night's rest, on Friday morning here we are ready for the awaited visit. From what I can tell it's not the first time this Porsche fan has been here, but it is a first for his son, who is with him. They have decided to take this first full day in Stuttgart for the museum visit, so that they can calmly enjoy it and take pictures of the many cars on view. They choose to do this, even though they know they will be returning on Saturday for the official inauguration of the exhibition about the sixty years of Porsche Clubs, which is the main motivation for this trip.

The day is spent pleasantly among some of the most representative cars in the brand's history, admiring with deserved attentiveness these 'living' witnesses of Porsche's deeds over the last decades. And I say 'living' because nearly all the cars on display are ready to run, kept in perfect shape by the technical services and the maintenance and restoration workshop, which can be seen at the end of the entrance hall behind a glass wall.

The cars on display are not always the same, since besides those that are more important and that rarely leave the museum, there are others that are switched out because Porsche has in its collection a quantity of cars far greater than the number they can show to the public, despite the large area available. The reason why cars frequently leave the museum is because they are going to participate in shows or classic car events in the most diverse locations, for the enjoyment of the many fans. Besides that, the museum often has temporary exhibits about certain events or themes, like the one that will be inaugurated tomorrow, ensuring that there is always something new and interesting on show, even for those who are repeat visitors.

But today there are many cars of interest to study and admire, even if they aren't exactly novelties. It is great to see again the Sascha, created by Ferdinand Porsche for the Targa Florio; the innovative Cisitalia projected to compete in Formula One; the simple 356/1, always beautiful and inspiring; the 356 Ferdinand offered to the Professor on his seventy-fifth birthday; a 356 SL identical to the one that participated for the first time in the 24 Hours of Le Mans; a magnificent blue 356 Speedster Carrera; the 718 that won the 12 Hours of Sebring in 1960; the winning 804 of the French Formula One Grand Prix in 1962; the 'miniscule' 909 of the hill climb races; the 908 that won the Targa Florio in 1969; an impressive sequence of 917s in diverse variants, including the prototype with the 16-cylinder engine, the 911 Panamericana … the list is long and allows one to get to know the history of the brand throughout the years and to validate personally the famous Porsche 'DNA'.

Now there is also a special space dedicated to 'Butzi' Porsche, who recently passed away,[41] paying homage to the one responsible for the design of the brand's most charismatic model, the 911, and also for the 904, by many considered to be the most beautiful Porsche ever. The memory of the Professor's grandson will forever be in the mind of the brand's lovers! It was among cars and memories of special moments that the first day of visit at the museum went by quickly. Now we could only anxiously wait for the next day, which promised much.

The Sascha designed by Ferdinand Porsche for the 1922 Targa Florio.

ABOVE: **Porsche 356/1 shines in its spot, 'proud' of being the forefather of the marque. Behind it is the Cisitalia – the Formula One car ordered by Piero Dusio, which was also built at Gmünd.**

RIGHT: **The 356 'Ferdinand' that was offered to Professor Porsche in 1950 celebrating his seventy-fifth birthday.**

A beutiful
356 Speedster
Carrera.

The famous
Fuhrmann
engine that
equipped the
356 Carreras
and the 550s.

The iconic 917 is very well represented in its several versions at the Porsche Museum.

The Panamericana that Ferry Porsche received on his eightieth birthday in 1989 is still a main attraction at the Porsche Museum.

Bright and early the next morning we pick up a beautiful Anthracite Brown Boxster S, which will be our very special means of transport for the next two days. The instructions are for us to be at the market place in Ludwigsburg, Zuffenhausen's neighbour 5 miles (8km) away, at the beginning of the afternoon, where all the participants in the sixty years of Porsche Clubs event will gather. As we have arrived before lunch, we decide to take the opportunity to walk around and enjoy the beautiful architecture of this pleasant city and especially of its majestic palace, against which many Porsches are photographed for official documents or magazines and books. We subsequently check out the gathering place, which in late morning is still occupied by the colourful local weekly market.

When we return after lunch, the market sellers and their stands have magically disappeared and now one can just see a couple of awnings occupied by Porsche Clubs Management staff that have started receiving the cars of the participants, guiding their parking in the wide market place. It quickly fills up with colour again, with beautiful cars either classic or more modern, but all of them proudly bearing the Porsche crest on their hood.

A very special detail – the Porsche crest designed in the tyre grooves.

The Marktplatz in Ludwigsburg receives the Porsche fans celebrating sixty years of Porsche Clubs.

It is a sight to see these machines as they arrive and we just have to look at the faces of the drivers and passengers to confirm their satisfaction at being here to celebrate sixty years of what we can consider to be a big family! This is where the members of the Porsche Clubs from several European countries and even some from the other side of the Atlantic get together and talk. Standing out are a couple of participants who are over ninety years of age, founding members of the Porsche Club of America. Meanwhile Hans-Peter Porsche also arrives, once again honouring the enthusiasts of the marque with his presence at this meeting. It is a notable tradition that has been maintained throughout the years, the direct involvement of members of the Porsche family at big and small events worldwide.

Sandra Mayr, director of the Porsche Clubs Management, requests the attention of all those attending, to explain the schedule of the events planned for this Saturday. We are to follow a route as a caravan with all the Porsches present here back to Zuffenhausen and to the museum, where the inauguration of the temporary exhibition dedicated to the clubs will take place. Part of the caravan is a very special Porsche, a red tractor[42] holding two flags showing the symbol of the brand.

Porsches gathered in Ludwigsburg leave the market square towards Zuffenhausen.

The caravan travels at reduced speed, catching the attention of people walking by, but when we arrive in Zuffenhausen a pleasant surprise is waiting for us. We are going into the Porsche Platz in front of the museum, but not through one of the normal public roads; instead, we will cross the streets inside the Werk II,[43]

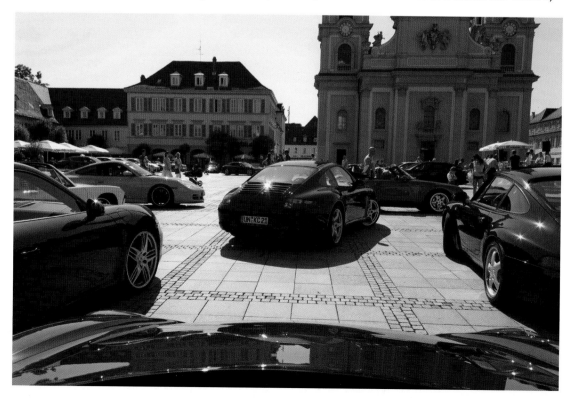

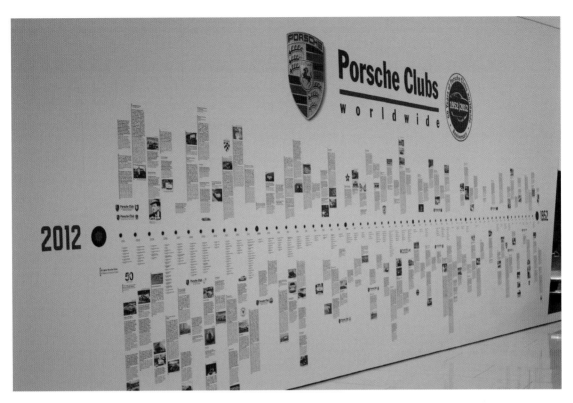

where almost all the Porsches present here were 'born', directly into the plaza through the main gate. It is a truly symbolic and unforgettable experience!

After passing in front of the museum we park the Boxster in the underground car park and head to the museum's main entrance, in front of which a group picture will be taken. Here there are some more moments to get together and there is a very special one for my 'host', when he has the opportunity to greet Hans-Peter Porsche and exchange some brief but meaningful words with him. I can really feel the importance and solemnity of this moment for the 'old' Porschist as he shakes the hand of the grandson of the Professor! It is a moment that he will never forget; and for me it is somewhat 'strange' and also very special.

After the photograph of the nearly 200 participants has been taken, it is time to go into the museum and enjoy the exhibition. After seeing a small film show-ing the creation of the Porsche Clubs, from the first[44] in 1952 until the present time, we then enjoy the mural that refers to all the clubs spread across the world, around 300, and the date of their creation. That first club was inaugurated on 26 May 1952 by seven Porsche owners, who expressed their motivation in the following way: 'to unite all Porsche drivers in friendship and in a comradely manner'.

Today, sixty years later, the almost 300 clubs total nearly 181,000 members in seventy-five countries. The biggest one is the Porsche Club of America, which consists of 107,000 members distributed amongst 137 regional clubs. There is no

Almost 300 Porsche Clubs created worldwide are named in this large mural at the museum.

other automobile brand that comes close to these amazing numbers and what they represent. At the exhibition, there is another mural with some interesting testimonies by members about their experiences as fans of the brand through their clubs. There are also a few showcases with diverse memorabilia alluding to the clubs and to events organized by them. In a nearby area, there are also some special limited-edition cars dedicated to some clubs, like the 996 Carrera S painted with a special colour, Azurro California Blue, celebrating the fifty years of the Porsche Club of America in 2005. Next to this car, there are others connected to other clubs and among them there is one covered with a white cloth, to which people are converging and where attention is now focused.

After welcoming speeches by Mathias Müller, Porsche's CEO, and by Bernhard Maier, the Marketing Director, it is now time to unveil the car built specially for this event. Mathias Müller and Bernhard Maier remove the white cover and there before everyone's eyes is a beautiful 991, painted Brewster Green (the favourite and almost exclusive colour of the Porsche family.) The inscriptions '911 Club Coupé' on the bottom of the door frames, the fine exclusive rims and the 'duck-tail' aileron on the engine cover stand out right away! The crowd applauds this wonderful car immediately; everyone is impressed by its beauty and exclusivity. In fact, only thirteen units will be made, with this first one destined to stay in the museum and with the twelve others being sold exclusively to Porsche Club members, with the right to buy it being subject to a lottery among those inter-

Mathias Müller, Hans-Peter Porsche and Bernhard Maier stand beside the 991 Club Coupé, which has been just revealed to the audience celebrating the sixty years of Porsche Clubs.

Mathias Müller shows the book that will be delivered to each of the fortunate twelve buyers of the special 991 Club Coupé.

ested. The lucky winners will have their name engraved on a small plaque fixed to the dashboard and will also be entitled to receive a book with photographs of the successive phases of the making of the car. It is now surrounded by many of the attendees, interested in taking a close-up look at some of the exterior details, as well as at its beautiful interior in shades of brown. It is without a doubt a fine machine, worthy of the brand's traditions and of the quality of work at the Porsche Exclusive Department, where the changes to this special model were designed and put into practice.

My 'host' is now closely admiring the Brewster Green paintwork (which changes its tone according to the light shining on it) and all of a sudden I feel an irresistible impulse to become part of the 911 Club Coupé, looking forward to different future experiences in the Porsche Exclusive Department or even in the Development Department at Weissach. All I need to do therefore is to wait for the habit my 'host' has of touching the cars that impress him so that I can make my move. And so it happens and moments later I say 'goodbye', thankful to this Porsche enthusiast that I accompanied for almost a year. But my objective has now been realized – I now have a very clear idea of what it is to be a fan of the brand and to feel a part of this great family. Good luck … and see you around!

I felt some nostalgia as I stepped away from the Club Coupé, maybe because of knowing that I could not become one of its privileged owners, but on the other hand very happy to have attended its presentation. Meanwhile, the scheduled events for the day continued with a commemorative dinner at the museum's restaurant, the famous 'Christophorus', which gathered all the participants in a cheerful and relaxed party environment. Curiously, destiny willed it that at our table sat Karl-Heinz Volz, General Director of Porsche Exclusive, and Boris Apenbrink, the project leader of the 911 Club Coupé! So we were able to get to know a bit better the department that tries to satisfy the special wishes of its clients regarding car customization.

On the next day, Sunday, there was a completely different programme, with a route of almost 56 miles (90km) to be driven. It would take us through beautiful rural roads to a wine-producing farm near Beilstein, where we would have lunch. We left the Porsche Platz and enjoyed the lovely villages and the scenery as we followed the directions on the road book, and suddenly, to our surprise we were in front of the Porsche facilities in Weissach. It was just a brief passage in front of the entrance building, but it was enough to realize how big the main development centre for the brand is, where the competition cars that have given their fans so much joy are designed and tested.

We kept going along our route and, having arrived at the destination, we parked in a grass field next to the farm's main building. The

Since 1952, the Porsche Clubs have been an important link between the brand and its customers. The anniversary commemorations in Zuffenhausen were a joyful and unforgettable mark in this unique relationship.

almost 100 cars from Zuffenhausen, lined up in four parallel rows, were a showcase of the many models produced throughout sixty years. It was interesting to compare, for example, a 356 Speedster from the 1950s with its most recent descendant based on the 997. Over five decades separated them, but it was clear that they were part of the same family – just a 'natural evolution of the species'.

After some pleasant hours spent in the rural environment of the farm, once again getting to know the other Porsche enthusiasts, the day and the event came to their end. We said goodbye to our kind hosts of the Porsche Club Management and drove back to Zuffenhausen. We enjoyed the trip back to the Porsche Platz, hearing the music of the flat-6 even better after we put the top down to appreciate the fresh breeze of the evening. When we arrived, we (regretfully) handed in the Boxster at the museum's garage and admired for the last time the magnificent architecture of the building, to which we hoped to return soon! Those three days remain in my memory as an unforgettable event, organized by Porsche once again in exemplary fashion.

4 SEPTEMBER 2013, NÜRBURGRING, GERMANY

Marc Lieb is seated at the wheel of the black 918 about to enter the Nürburgring Nordschleife circuit. The aim is clear: to establish the fastest lap for a production street-legal vehicle fitted with standard tyres. Porsche wants to prove how well ahead of the competition it is with its 918 with hybrid technology.

After receiving the order to enter the track, given by Dr Frank Walliser, 918 project director, Marc Lieb starts confidently, taking advantage of the first kilometres until the timing line to scan all systems and prepare for the intense 13 miles (20.8km) that follow. Past the timing line, near the connection to the modern Formula One circuit, Lieb accelerates decidedly and the roar of the V8 invades the cockpit, projecting the 918 forwards under heavy acceleration. Immediately afterwards, the brakes are applied for the first time (generating electricity to charge the batteries), since the initial part of the circuit is quite winding until Hocheichen. Then again, a strong acceleration to Flugplatz, with Lieb lifting his right foot a little, to avoid a big jump that could destabilize the car, then accelerating immediately afterwards, allowing us to reach Schwedenkreuz at more than 186.45mph (300km/h). This is followed by heavy braking into the right curve of Aremberg, then acceleration uphill to Adenauer-Forst.

The 918 has an extraordinary power of acceleration when the power of the V8 (608bhp) is joined to the instantly available torque of its two electric motors (one in each axle), which offers 286bhp more, enabling the car to reach 218mph (351km/h). Thus it can make the most of any small section of straight between the demanding curves. Lieb dominates the 918 perfectly and without great effort,

as it responds brilliantly to his driving and only very rarely can any protest from the tyres be heard, which clearly proves the dynamic qualities of the chassis built entirely in carbon-fibre and developed in Weissach.

Now we arrive at Ex-Mühle, braking for this left turn over the small bridge and immediately Lieb accelerates towards the right turn of Bergwerk, after which the sound of the V8 can be heard again in its fullness, allowing speeds close to 186.42mph (300km/h) in this less twisting section. Then we have to brake for the corners that precede the famous Karussell, which we negotiate quickly at about 56mph (90km/h) on the inside, as usual.

Four minutes have passed since the start of the lap and we are going towards the difficult turns of Eschbach, Brünnchen and Eiskurve, where the 918 shows its excellent balance and traction power again. Some seconds later we are on the small Karussell, from which we exit with Lieb searching for the ideal path to tackle the right curve of Galgenkopf, leading to the longer straight of the circuit, the Döttinger Höhe, where we again reach the high speeds the 918 can easily deal with.

We quickly arrive at Tiergarten and to the final corners before the finish line, which Lieb negotiates nimbly. The time indicated on the display panel is a fantastic 6 minutes 57 seconds when the 918 reaches the finish line and stops the timing system. The whole technical team celebrates the fantastic achievement

ABOVE AND OPPOSITE: **Marc Lieb drives the 918 on the Nürburgring Nordschleife, committed to setting a new lap record.**

The Porsche team celebrates a fantastic new lap record for a production street-legal car at the Nürburgring – an astonishing 6min 57sec.

and salutes Marc Lieb, who stops immediately afterwards, pleased with himself and with the fantastic supercar that has just beaten the previous record by no less than 14 seconds! For me to 'live' this historical record will certainly remain an unforgettable milestone. What an extraordinary journey and how great the technological development has been since the days when I discovered this wonderful circuit for first time aboard the small 550.

The Nürburgring has been from the beginning of Porsche's saga deeply attached to its history and has had a special significance for those responsible for the brand and for its drivers, but also for its fans. A few days after the magnificent record was set, Porsche returned to celebrate at the Nordschleife with the 918 and the fastest car to run on this circuit, the 962, which in 1983 established a mark that even today seems impossible: 6min 11sec, at the hands of the 'prince of speed', Stefan Bellof, who unfortunately passed by this planet only fleetingly but brilliantly, like a fascinating comet.

On that date, 28 May 1983, during practice for the 1,000km race, the 962 was driven as never previously, with it seeming that an alien had taken the wheel, so much so that the Porsche staff did not immediately realize Stefan Bellof's feat, because they were waiting for him to complete his lap around 10 seconds later. Klaus Bischoff could not believe it when Bellof got out of the car and the admiration was such that they were looking at each other without saying a single word for long seconds. Everything had already been said!

DECEMBER 2013, ZUFFENHAUSEN, GERMANY/ JANUARY 2014, BRUSSELS, BELGIUM

After being in the Porsche Exclusive Department at the factory and the Development Department at Weissach, where I was able to follow the last part of the development of the 918, I have decided to try to find my 'friend' (I think I can call him that!) who brought me back to Zuffenhausen during the celebrations for the sixty years of the Porsche Clubs. The main reason for my decision is the fact that at the time I had heard him talking to his son about wanting to write a book about Porsche!

When I thought in depth about this subject, I realized that I would also really enjoy telling my adventures connected to the marque, after having been, by chance or fate, 'made part of' the 60K10. But I quickly concluded that I would need a 'middleman' to whom I could 'transmit' my stories, so that he could then put them on paper. And to that effect the 'old Porschist' would definitely be the right person and I believe I can be a good help so that he can achieve his goal too.

The great difficulty is now being able to find him again and putting myself in position for our 'symbiosis' to happen again. So, I decided to transfer back to the museum, where I started paying attention to the conversations about events to which Porsche would send cars, hoping that destiny would also take my 'friend' to one of them so that our paths would cross again.

Steffan Bellof in a 956 did an 'extra-terrestrial' lap at the Nürburgring Nordschleife during practice for the 1983 1,000km.

The next great event is at the Autoworld in Brussels, where there will be a big exhibition: 'Ferdinand Porsche, The Heritage, from Electric to Electric'. This exhibit will pay homage to the four Ferdinands and to the automobiles created by them, starting with the creations of Professor Ferdinand Porsche, long before the marque was born. It will be a unique event, since besides cars coming from the museum in Zuffenhausen, there will be many others that belong to other organizations or private collectors, with the 'crown jewel' being the only surviving 60K10 of the three built in 1939, which is rarely seen in public. I bet my Porschist 'friend', if he knows about this exhibit, will be there!

Now, I needed to know which cars the museum intended to send, in order to 'catch a ride' on one of them. It wasn't very difficult to get that information, and I set my sights on the Cisitalia, the Formula One project developed for the Italian marque in 1946/48. It will be on show in Brussels and maybe not very far from the 60K10. It has not been easy, but after several 'moves' within the museum I managed to achieve my goal, right on the eve of the Cisitalia's departure to Brussels.

The Cisitalia at the Autoworld exhibition in Brussels.

After being offloaded at the Autoworld and taken to the place of the exhibition, to my excitement I can see that the 60K10 is already here. The cars are not in their

Otto Mathé in the 60K10 at a road race in Korneuburg (1952).

Otto Mathé in the 60K10 at another road race in Linz (1952).

definitive spots yet because the scenery is still being finished. Now I have to count on the contribution of the team of workers placing the cars in their respective spots, in order to migrate successfully to the 60K10. After some hours of waiting and paying attention to the movements, I manage it. Here I am now in this 'old acquaintance', the third unit built of the 60K10, which became famous for the many races it competed in while driven (with only one hand!)[45] by the Austrian Otto Mathé. The opening of the show is tomorrow and here I will be waiting for a very special visitor!

Many days have gone by since the opening of the exhibition on 6 December and I'm starting to have some doubts about the success of my mission, as my much awaited visitor has not appeared. The exhibition has been a success, with a lot of visitors admiring the cars on display, but it is now the last day of the event, Sunday, 19 January, and I confess that I'm a little nervous, though I still hope that my 'friend' will appear 'in the nick of time'.

It is now some minutes past 10:30 and I look at the visitors that pass by the 60K10, expecting to find someone I recognize ... and suddenly I can see in the distance a person walking quickly past the other cars without really looking at them, heading this way with quick and sure steps. No, it doesn't look like him ... but he is now closer and when I can see him more clearly I'm sure – yes, it is my 'old Porschist'! I see him pulling his camera out of its bag and taking photos from all angles of the 60K10. His joy is evident at seeing 'live' for the first time this pioneer of the Porsche design and 'DNA'. He is now asking another visitor to take a picture of him next to the car. After that, he calmly enjoys all the details, going around the 60K10 several times. Suddenly I remember that if he doesn't touch the bodywork I won't be able to fulfil my wish, but I'm sure he'll do it!

And in fact it doesn't take too long, as, shortly after, following an irresistible impulse, he passes his hand lightly over the fender, making it slide smoothly and giving me enough time to go from the metallic environment to the biological. The built-up energy is dissipated in a small electrical discharge and ... it's done! Now we will see if in the near future I can transmit my adventures, 'inspiring' my friend to write his so-desired book ...

30 MAY 2014, SINTRA, PORTUGAL

It's a little past 09:00 when we arrive at the beautiful town of Sintra, which today will be visited by the participants of the thirty-ninth 356 International Meeting. These encounters, organized by the Porsche Classic Clubs department, are held every year in the most diverse countries, gathering together many beautiful units of Porsche's first-series production model. This year it fell on Porsche Club 356 Portugal to organize the event and of course my 'friend' could not pass up this opportunity to enjoy so many rarities, even though he is already quite busy with the preparation and writing of his book.

Even though it is quite early, it will be hard to find a place to park and we go through the narrow streets of the town unsuccessfully. After a steep descent, we see a sign pointing to a park, but at its entrance there is a police officer and we realize that the park is reserved for the participants of the event, who have yet to arrive. We stop, but unexpectedly the officer signals us in, possibly thinking that the 944 is the first car to arrive. After we explain that we are not participants, but rather spectators looking for a place to park, the officer hesitates and contacts a colleague on the radio, who arrives in less than a minute on his motorcycle. To our surprise, the officer says he can get us a spot without interfering with the ones that are reserved for the 356s. So, thankful and touched, my 'friend' follows the officer's motorcycle to the spot he indicates, next to two of the organization's cars. With great excitement, we realize we will be really close to the venerable Porsche forefathers.

There will be almost 200 356s distributed in three parking lots throughout the small town, giving it lots of colour and a bustle far greater than usual! The cars will be distributed in the parks according to their age and we're now going to the park of the oldest ones, which naturally are given the best location, right in front of the Palácio Nacional de Sintra, itself an ancient site, since it dates from the thirteenth century.

When we get there after walking for a few minutes, the first 356s are arriving and our admiration increases by the minute as the row of wonderful cars grows.

A line-up of 356s at the 2014 International Meeting in Sintra, Portugal.

**Two beautiful
356 Speedsters.**

There are already six Speedsters! And also several Pre-As (the oldest from 1951), both Coupés and Cabriolets. There are even some Carreras, whose sound upon arrival naturally turns heads and fuels the dreams of some of those attending. It is a real showcase of the diversity of models to come out of the Zuffenhausen factory in the first ten years of production.

**A 356 Pre-A
Coupé from
1951.**

ABOVE: **A fantastic 356 Pre-A Cabriolet from 1951 ...**

... and its pristine dashboard.

**A superb 356
Cabriolet from
1952.**

As to the places where they come from, one can see via the licence plates that most of them naturally come from several European countries, with a predominance of Germany, but there are also those that have come from the USA, South Africa and even from Australia, giving a very international look to this wonderful event.

After having gone through two parks with many points of interest, we return to the one where we left the 944 that is now surrounded (and honoured!) by distinguished and colourful company. In this park are the most recent 356s, most of them being type C.

The morning goes by quickly and now the 356s start leaving the parking lots, moving as a caravan to a nearby wine cellar, where lunch will be served to their drivers and companions. We get the chance to visit this place as well, in order to take some more photographs. We see that it is a very convivial atmosphere, where participants can refresh themselves and embark on lively conversations with fellow owners about the adventures they have had in their marvellous machines. It is impressive how well kept these cars are, as almost all of them are over fifty years old and some of them more than sixty. Indeed, it is at an event like this that we realize it is perfectly possible for the marque's claim to be true that two-thirds of all Porsches are still in circulation!

Another parking area in Sintra with a lot of 356 Cs that travelled from many different countries to the 2014 356 International Meeting.

Regretfully, we have to leave such interesting company and return home, but we are quite happy with what we have seen. It is moments like these that feed and reinforce the passion of many Porsche enthusiasts, whether they are participating in the events or just enjoying them as enthusiastic spectators.

Sintra, a small and beautiful Portuguese town, was full of Porsche cars, creating a very special atmosphere for the local people, Porsche enthusiasts and visitors.

10–15 JUNE 2015, CIRCUIT DE LA SARTHE, LE MANS, FRANCE

I'm not at the de la Sarthe circuit – since I opted to accompany my Porsche enthusiast 'friend' in the writing of his book, I can't experience this great event live, where the fans of the brand are anxiously awaiting a hopeful return to victory after seventeen years of 'fasting'. The last victory, in 1998, was achieved by the Laurent Aïello/Allan McNish/Stéphane Ortelli team with a 911 GT3.[46] Porsche only came back to compete at Le Mans at the highest level in 2014 with the revolutionary 919 hybrid, which, even though it led the race briefly, finished in eleventh place after experiencing some mechanical problems.

But after this 'learning year', Porsche has come back with a redoubled will to attain the most important win in the race calendar. This year it reinforces its chances by bringing three 919s: no.17 with Timo Bernhard, Brendon Hartley and Mark Webber; no.18 with Marc Lieb, Romain Dumas and Neel Jani; and no.19 with Earl Bamber, Nick Tandy and Nico Hulkenberg. The cars form a flashy group, each one painted in its own colour: red for no.17; black for no.18; and white for no.19. The main adversaries will be Audi (with three R18 e-tron Quattros), which has dominated the race in the last few years, and Toyota (with two TS040s), which is anxiously looking for its first victory in the most prestigious race in automotive sport.

The Porsche team prepared to fight for a seventeeth victory at the 24 Hours of Le Mans.

Even though I'm not at Le Mans, I won't miss any part of the emotions of the race, because my 'friend' will watch it from start to finish, as is his habit. Today is still Wednesday, but the television is already on, awaiting the start of the first free practice session. The first images show us the inside of the Toyota and Audi pits, but next to the stoplight, already waiting to get out on the track, are the 919s, among the strange front-engined Nissan cars. Once again, the bustle at the Le Mans circuit begins and, even though they're just practice sessions and despite the fact that we are 1,000 miles (1,600km) away, we can already feel the emotion that the legendary race causes in its enthusiasts!

The Porsche cars go through the start/finish straight for the first time. It is wet, since it rained before the start of this practice session. We can already see images inside the cockpit of the no.17 919 driven by Mark Webber. The environment around the driver in these modern cars is quite different to when I was last able to take part at the end of the 1990s. There are lights and buttons everywhere, on the steering wheel and on the dashboard, as well as screens with multiple bits of information for the driver. Driving is no longer just a steering wheel, three pedals and a gear lever, to go as fast as you can! Now one has to deal also with energy management, charging batteries, megajoules and regenerative braking, a technical paraphernalia that would be hard to imagine a decade ago. But it is impressive that all this technology gives the 919s' drivers 1,000bhp (or even a bit more than that) with a main engine that is only a 2-litre V4!

We now have images of the track from the no.18 Porsche and it is with some nostalgia that I see the familiar scenery passing by at great speed: Hunaudières, Mulsanne, Indianapolis, Arnage, Porsche Curves, the Ford Chicane and the start/finish straight. After 4 hours, the free practice comes to an end and we check the results: the no.17 Porsche gets the best time with 3min 21.36sec, followed by the best of the Audi cars just 0.58sec behind, with the no.18 919 in third place. Not bad to start, but this was just an appetizer. We will see how the first timed practice session will go starting at 22:00.

And here we are at the scheduled time. Night is falling on the circuit and the row of cars waiting for the green light so as to get out on the track is long. The green comes on and off they go for 2 hours of fighting for a good time! The red 919 is already charging, followed closely from the pits with the full attention of Porsche's technical staff, drivers and mechanics. There are now images from the inside of the no.18 919 with Neel Jani at the wheel and we can tell that he is on a pretty fast lap. We wait for him to pass the finish line and there it is, 3min 16.89sec, almost 5 seconds less than the time they had taken in the afternoon. The hostilities have begun! This time beats the track record by 2 seconds.

The no.17 919 now comes into the pit, the front hood is replaced (maybe with a different aerodynamic kit) and Brendon Hartley goes out on the track looking for a good result. At the end of 1 hour of practice, there is no news as to the best time and now there is even a red flag, due to two accidents, with all the cars returning to the pits. The three best times belong to the Porsche 919s. With 34 minutes to go until the end of the session, there is a green light once again and the cars go back to the track to try to improve their positions. All the teams are interested in getting a good time today, since there is the possibility of rain for the next qualifying session on Thursday.

Romain Dumas is being interviewed, showing his satisfaction with the results obtained so far and hoping to get the win in the race, which he has won once but wishes to do so again with a Porsche. There are now 2 minutes left to the end of the session and there are no cars among the best trying to improve their times. It seems that Audi and Toyota are now convinced that, at least for today, the Porsches are unbeatable. So midnight comes and the chequered flag is shown, with the session coming to an end with the three Porsches in the lead. The best of the Audi cars is in fourth position, almost 3 seconds away from the best Porsche, and the best Toyota is seventh, over 6.5sec behind the provisional pole position time. The first day of practice sessions has gone well for Porsche.

On Thursday, we also follow the practice session, but there are no improvements in times for the major contenders, so Porsche succeeds in getting its cars in the first three positions of the starting grid. After the end of the session, the feeling among the drivers is of great excitement as they pose for the customary photograph with 'Miss 24 Heures du Mans' and for the first page of Le Maine Libre, *announcing Porsche's feat.*

Finally, the day of the race is here. It is 08:00 and we are already watching the warm-up, which the teams take advantage of to test and fine-tune the definitive settings to use in the race. The Porsche cars go out on track immediately and we are very hopeful that everything will go well, foreshadowing a good race. The determined hour for the warm-up goes by quickly and without any mishaps. All that is left now is to wait anxiously for 15:00 and the commencement of the great excitement of the race!

There are 15 minutes to go to the start and we're enjoying the bustle along the starting grid. On the first row there are the 919s, the black no.18 and the red no.17, that together with no.19 will certainly give all they've got to be in front by the end of the race. Brendon Hartley is saying that the race will certainly be well disputed and really fast.

The fifty-four cars turn their engines on and start moving for the formation lap. The magic of the 24 Hours of Le Mans is about to begin! The cars are zigzagging, warming up their tyres behind the pace car, and the first ones are now at the end of the Mulsanne Straight. Besides the 919s there are naturally more Porsches enrolled in the two GT categories, amongst which the beautiful GT3 Cup of Patrick Dempsey's team stands out, driven by him, Patrick Long and Marco Seefried.

The focus is doubled now, as the pack arrives at the chicane before the start/

finish straight, the pace car leaves the track and the flag is waved to start the race, the drivers 'release' the thousands of horsepower from their machines and off they go! The two Porsches of the front row stay side by side until the end of the straight and when the cars reach the Dunlop Bridge, the three 919s are in the lead, followed by the Audis and the Toyotas. Before they get to the first chicane on the Mulsanne Straight, Timo Bernhard in the red 919, nicknamed the 'Red Baron', goes into the lead, overtaking the black 919 (the 'Black Knight') and the competition during the braking amongst the leaders is close. It seems that we are in a sprint race and not a 24-hour one!

The cars are quickly passing Indianapolis and brake to deal with the Arnage corner, accelerating almost like dragsters as they exit towards the Porsche Curves. Again we have them at the Ford Chicane, with Bernhard holding first position. The Audis are attacking and Loïc Duval overtakes Nico Hulkenberg in the braking and grabs the third position. They all go into the start/finish straight going over and beyond the kerbs, fighting closely for position. The two Porsches are still in front, but the Audis keep attacking, occupying now the third and fourth places.

The times of the front-running cars on the second lap are between 3min 21sec and 3min 22sec, showcasing the unrelenting fight that is happening. By the end of five laps, the first six runners fit within 7 seconds! We're now momentarily inside Timo Bernhard's 919, which is already passing the last of the GT cars. He does so courageously and decisively, almost as if they were not there, so as to lose the minimum amount of time.

The no.19 Porsche comes into the pit, after 34 minutes of racing, for its first refuelling, at the same time as one of the Audis. On the next lap, the no.18 919 and the no.7 Audi come in and apparently everything is going as planned. The leader is still Bernhard in the 'Red Baron'; he is also making his first pit stop now. After the first stint for the main protagonists, the two Porsches are still leading, almost 'glued' to each other and gaining time over the pursuing Audis and the Toyotas that are behind them.

Thanks to modern technology, we can follow the race not only on television, but also via a tablet we can watch the race from inside any car of the main teams. Of course, my 'friend' chooses mostly one of the front-running Porsches. We are also keeping track of the times, standings and pit stops on a computer. We are only missing the fabulous sound of the cars, the smell of petrol and burnt rubber – but one can't have it all!

The first hour of racing has been completed with the Porsches in the lead, but the Audis are still coming on strong. Meanwhile, there is a scare when we see one of the factory Porsches of the GTE-Pro category being hit by a Rebellion, catch fire and be forced to retire. But this year the expectations of the Porsche fans are all focused on the LMP1 class, leaving what goes on in other categories in the background.

The safety cars[47] come on to the track so that it can be cleaned and there is a quieter period, allowing for a slight 'decompression' inside and outside the cars. This period lasts slightly over 20 minutes, then everything is restarted, with Nico Hulkenberg standing out as he decisively attacks the Audis in front of him and overtakes Loïc Duval spectacularly as they enter the Porsche Curves.

The first six runners are all together, with a slight advantage (under 2 seconds) for Timo Bernhard, who is still in the lead. But on the following lap, there is an unexpected turn of events in the lead, as André Lotterer in the no.7 Audi attacks heavily and is able to pass the two Porsches between the Dunlop Chicane and the Tertre Rouge turn. Bernhard reacts and tries to recover first position, but the Audi driver is resisting well. In the next lap, Bernhard, pressured by Neel Jani, misses the braking for the first Hunaudières chicane and relinquishes second place to the Swiss driver.

After an hour and a half of racing, the fight for the first positions is still strong in all the classes and the second set of refuelling begins. The leading Audi makes the scheduled pit stop and Timo Bernhard returns to the lead, performing two laps with times around 3min 19sec, trying to gain as much time as possible until he makes his second trip into the pits for refuelling. When he returns to the track he is able to keep first place, but when the second hour of racing ends it is the no.7 Audi that is in front, followed by the three Porsches.

The continuation of an extremely close race is anticipated. We're sure to get our fair share of suffering throughout the long hours ahead of us! A decisive factor may come at the third pit stop – it's speculated that the Audis are able to do four stints with the same tyres, unlike the Porsches, which can only manage to do three. After the pit stops of the 919s, that situation is confirmed, which may become a problem for the Porsches if they lose more time in the pits throughout the race.

Thus the Audi of André Lotterer has retaken the lead and now has a 28 second advantage over the no.17 Porsche, currently being driven by Brendon Hartley. But shortly after, surprise – the leading Audi returns to the pits after having driven only three laps and switches tyres and driver. It seems this unexpected situation was due to a flat tyre, but what matters is that the 'Red Baron' is out in front once again.

When we are almost three hours into the race we get a scare when in a pack of LMP1 cars overtaking GT's there is an LMP1, seemingly a Porsche, that loses control and hits the guard rails violently; but no, it's the no.8 Audi of Loïc Duval, which loses its front end but manages to come back on track to get to the pits and repair the damage. Now there are two Audis with significant time losses. The Audi's accident also led to a safety-car period to allow for the repair of the guard rails.

As the third hour passes, the three Porsches 919s are leading in the order of their race numbers. Will it continue? Is Porsche on the way to its seventeenth victory? After over half an hour of safety cars the racers are once again 'set free' and due to the fact that the no.17 919 stayed behind one safety car, and the no.18 along with the Audis behind another one, the difference between the two Porsches is 1min 15sec.

We get to the end of the fourth hour still with Hartley in the lead, followed now by the no.9 Audi 11.4 seconds behind him, with Filipe Albuquerque behind the wheel, then the no.7 Audi with Benoît Tréluyer and after him the other two Porsches. Albuquerque is pressing hard, breaking the lap record twice and setting it on 3min 16.64sec. His Audi is now tailgating the leading Porsche. He puts as much pressure as possible on for two laps, but is unable to overtake and is now coming into the pits to refuel. However, the Audis have just shown that they can go very fast and put up a fight with the Porsches!

By the end of the fifth hour of racing the situation out in front is holding, with an advantage from the no.17 Porsche to the Audi of only 10.7sec. The other 919s are in the fourth and fifth positions, followed by the two Toyota cars already one lap behind the leaders. When at 20:30 Brendon Hartley comes into the pits at the end of three stints and hands the car over to Mark Webber, Filipe Albuquerque in the no.9 Audi climbs into the first position. When he stops 10 minutes later, Audi's advantage is confirmed when he sets off for his fourth stint without having changed tyres.

With the sixth hour completed, it is the 'Red Baron' that is briefly in the lead, but it will have to give in to the no.7 Audi of Benoît Tréluyer when it stops to refuel shortly afterwards.

We are approaching the end of the seventh hour of the race and night begins to settle in. The headlights are drawing trajectories on the track, but they make identification of the cars harder. It is a festival of lights both on and off the circuit, which has an actual fair around it. The long night at Le Mans is about to begin!

Nico Hulkenberg/ Nick Tandy/ Earl Bamber with the 919 no.19 was the youngest Porsche team enrolled to compete in the 2015 24 Hours of Le Mans.

At seven hours of racing, when the no.17 Porsche comes into the pit, the no.9 Audi goes back into the lead, now driven by René Rast. Suddenly there is another scare, as the no.18 919 with Romain Dumas at the wheel goes straight ahead at the end of the Hunaudières, hitting the tyre wall, though fortunately only softly and it carries on with the race. Immediately in the pits a new front section for the 'Black Knight' is made ready and when it calls in the front is quickly replaced, using the stop to change tyres and driver too. Neel Jani is now at the wheel. This incident cost the team some time, but despite this it has remained in fifth position behind the no.19 919 of Nico Hulkenberg.

The fight for the first positions is reflected in the current standings, in which the Porsches occupy first, third and fifth positions, with the Audis in second, fourth and sixth, followed by the two Toyotas. Any prognosis as to the victory at the end of the race is risky!

It's now 23:00 and we're past the first third of the race, with the safety cars on the track again due to an accident. This time the leaders are all together and waiting for more action! After the exit of the safety cars the hostilities are restarted and after the pit stops by the no.9 Audi and the no.17 Porsche, it is now the no.19 919 that steps into the lead for the first time. Thus, by the end of just over 8 hours of racing, all three Porsches have been in the lead. My 'friend' and I are still in a very good mood and willing to follow the adventures of this extraordinary race through the night and into the dawn!

By 23:30, there is an announcement that Mark Webber, who has been leading the race, has to stop in the pits to serve a 1 minute penalty due to overtaking in a yellow flag area. The no.7 Audi that is following him stops at the same time and because of that Hulkenberg gets back into first position. The no.17 919 will have to return to the pits in the next lap for its regular stop to refuel and change tyres. These two consecutive stops may have compromised the red no.17 919's race.

But the young drivers of the third car that Porsche brought to Le Mans are doing very well. Nico Hulkenberg, Earl Bamber and Nick Tandy are on their second race with the 919 and for the first two it is their first time at the 24 Hours of Le Mans. So the white 919, whose nickname I don't know but which I'm going to start calling 'White Lady', is not experiencing problems or setbacks and is now in front of its sister cars, leading the race. The leaders are still lapping with times between 3min 18sec and 3min 20sec, a real sprint-worthy pace. Hulkenberg attacks before the pit stop and manages to increase his lead over Fassler to almost 30 seconds..

In the following 2 hours, the lead of the race alternates between the no.19 Porsche and the no.7 and no.9 Audis according to their pit stops. At 01:07, we see the 'Black Knight' of Neel Jani exit the track again in the Mulsanne area and hit the tyre barrier relatively slowly. There is not much damage and after 3 minutes the 919 gets back on track, headed to the pits, where the front is replaced and

Marc Lieb steps in behind the wheel. After this incident, among the Porsches only the 'White Lady' is still having a totally problem-free race.

Until the middle of the race at 03:00 the suspense continues, since the cars in front continue to alternate positions when they stop in the pits and the standings are as follows:

- *first – Porsche 919 no.19 (Nick Tandy)*
- *second – Audi no.9 (Marco Bonanomi) + 1min 3sec*
- *third – Audi no.7 (André Lotterer) + 1min 9sec*
- *fourth – Porsche no.17 (Brendon Hartley) + one lap*
- *fifth – Audi no.8 (Loïc Duval) + one lap*
- *sixth – Porsche no.18 (Marc Lieb) + two laps*

Nick Tandy is consistently lapping between 3min 19sec and 3min 20sec, increasing his lead as the Audis seem to be unable to keep up with these lap times now that the temperature has gone down. It is also noteworthy that during the night the Porsche can now do four driving stints with the same set of tyres, proving their greater efficiency with these temperatures. But there is no doubt that with 12 hours of racing still ahead anything can happen, with the gaps among the leaders being almost irrelevant.

It is now 05:30 and the sky is starting to turn blue, announcing the sunrise. The no.19 919 now driven by Earl Bamber comes into the pit, stops and … oh no! The mechanics get the skates under the car and are going to take it into the garage … but thankfully it's a false alarm. They are just putting it in the right place for refuelling, as it has not been able to line up properly due to the movement in the contiguous pit. What a relief! After refuelling, it leaves the pit lane and is immediately behind the no.7 Audi.

The day is getting brighter and the most difficult part of the race for the drivers (and for us!) is thankfully past. We all stood up to the stress quite well! In fact, the suspense, adrenalin and magic of the night at Le Mans give the strength needed to the drivers, mechanics and spectators to resist until the end of the 24hr.

At 06:00, after 15 hours of racing, the 'White Lady' is still in first place with a 55-second lead over the no.7 Audi and 2 minutes over the no.9 Audi. The 'Red Baron' is still in the fight for the first places, being in fourth position.

There are now 5 minutes to go until 07:00 and unexpectedly the no.7 Audi loses part of its bodywork and comes into the pits for repairs. The Audi loses 7 minutes in the pits for the repairs and replacement of the rear hood. The Porsches' most dangerous adversary is now further away from a possible victory!

With two-thirds of the race done, Nico Hulkenberg, who is now at the wheel of the no.19 Porsche, keeps first place with a one-lap lead over the no.9 Audi of René Rast. There are still 8 hours to go in this race, which is still more than a regular Championship race and among the Porsche people the satisfaction and confidence in a good result are evident.

At 07:42, the safety cars come back on track after an accident and the first four runners are all together, though the first two are still separated by one lap. Meanwhile, the 919 that is in the lead has to come into the pits for its regular stop, still with the safety car on track. We fear the worst, when this time we actually see it go into the garage, with the rear hood being removed, but fortunately it is out again after 1 minute. However, there is suspense again, as it is held at the red light before entering the track, since it has to wait for the next safety car to come by to get behind it. It's nerve-wracking because with such a close race these involuntary stopping times might be decisive. Fortunately, Nick Tandy, who has taken Hulkenberg's place, is only held slightly over 1 minute before being able to set off and defend his premier position.

After 20 minutes of limited racing, the safety cars leave the track and Mark Webber in the 'Red Baron' immediately passes the no.9 Audi. There are now two Porsches leading the 24 Hours of Le Mans. The 919 of Nick Tandy is 2min 7sec ahead of its sister car of Mark Webber and 2min 10sec ahead of the no.9 Audi of René Rast. The odds of winning are increasing, as is both the excitement and anxiety among the fans!

Between 08:00 and 11:00 the situation remains stable, only varying slightly according to the pit stops, and the only alarm is when Timo Bernhard, overtaking a GT at the end of the start/finish straight, goes on to the gravel at great speed. However, he manages to avoid damage to the car since it flew really low, barely touching the gravel. He re-enters the track at the Dunlop Chicane, handling masterfully a situation that could have been quite delicate.

We are now 10 minutes away from 13:00, so nearly 2 hours away from the finish of the race, and the no.7 Audi, which is the only one that is still putting up a fight with the Porsches, goes into the pits and is pushed into the garage. The rear hood is removed and some checks are made. Bernard Tréluyer, who has replaced André Lotterer, leaves the garage after slightly over 1 minute and gets back on track. Because of that, the situation is a little better for Porsche, and even more so when the Audi comes back into the pits on the next lap to correct something that wasn't well resolved in the previous stop. Our trust in victory increases and my 'friend' is more and more convinced that Porsche will bring him great joy today.

At 13:25, Earl Bamber brings the 919 into the pits once more, to refuel and change tyres. He hands the steering wheel over to Nico Hulkenberg for the final stint. What is going through Hulkenberg's head, in this special moment in which he must accept the responsibility of driving the last hour and a half at Le Mans, without making mistakes and keeping the car in one piece until the end? We are all with him, wishing that everything goes well.

With 1 hour to go, the two 919s are still in front, with Hulkenberg in the 'White Lady' one lap ahead of Hartley in the 'Red Baron' and two laps ahead of the no.7

Audi. Everything seems to be going in Porsche's favour, but we must anxiously await 15:00 and the last lap. This final hour will be a terribly long one!

It is now 14:11 and the no.19 Porsche comes into the pits to refuel, perhaps for the last time, and it is with relief that we see it set off again for the final stage. The emotion increases when we see in the pits Dr Wolfgang Porsche and Mathias Müller, with their eyes glued to the screens, anxious but confident about the final results. The tradition is maintained and Wolfgang Porsche even shows the cameras his fingers crossed on his left hand! The stands in front of the pits are full and many Porsche flags are now starting to be seen in the hands of fans.

When there are just 15 minutes to go until 15:00 there is another little hiccough – Nico Hulkenberg brings the 919 into the pits again! But it is just a 'splash and dash' to get some fuel in the tanks, as a precautionary measure for the last laps. After a few minutes, to the surprise of some, Dr Ullrich, the director of Audi Motorsports, cordially visits the Porsche pit to greet and congratulate his opposition on this long marathon – an honourable gesture.

There are now 5 minutes left until the chequered flag and with the two 919s in front, it is practically impossible for victory to elude the Stuttgart-Zuffenhausen brand. Wolfgang Porsche and Fritz Enzinger, the director of the LMP1 programme, are talking and smiling now that success is so close. Mathias Müller shows a T-shirt painted with the number 17 inside a crown made of laurels and the inscription 'Porsche – 2015', with 'Mission: Future Sportscar, Challenge

The Porsche 919 hybrid no.19 did not experience any problems during the race, maintaining an impressive pace the whole time.

Accepted' written on the back. The ambience is now one of great joy among all those present in the pit, where one can see all the drivers of the 919 that have already finished their 'work' hanging out together.

This is the last lap and the communication to Nico Hulkenberg is heard, asking him to slow down a bit to allow Brendon Hartley to get closer, so that, as is the tradition, they can cross the finish line together. By the time they get to the Porsche Curves the two 919s are together. And it is clear how emotional Wolfgang Porsche is … his damp eyes reveal his state of mind!

Many mechanics, Porsche personnel and fans are now coming to the pit-lane wall with their flags to celebrate the victory and salute the drivers. The 919s can be seen arriving at the chicanes before the start/finish straight, driving by in front of the Porsche Experience Centre, its terrace crowded with fans who greet them with dozens of flags, rejoicing with the victory. Almost immediately, they are on the straight, with no.19 closer to the wall and no.17 beside it. The excitement and happiness in those who have come to greet them is enormous and that's how the cars receive the chequered flag, with many of the brand's flags being enthusiastically waved by the fans as they pass by. (At my 'friend's' house there is also a flag that has been kept for a long time, for this special occasion!)

Porsche has just won the 24 Hours of Le Mans for the seventeeth time! The announced return to competitions and great victories is now in full effect. There are hugs and tears of joy in the Porsche pits. The reward for all the work done in the last two years is finally here!

Nico Hulkenberg has just finished the 2015 24 Hours of Le Mans in the victorious 919 no.19, getting the seventeeth win in the famous race for Porsche, signifying its return to motor-sport endurance competition at the highest level.

Without a doubt, this was a great victory for Porsche, both in the sports field and in the technical field, since the 919 is in fact an amalgam of technology. None of its adversaries dared to risk so much!

The 919 project was announced on 12 June 2012, with the declared intention to return to competition at its highest level in 2014. The car would be a hybrid developed according to the ACO regulations for the LMP1 category. The technical novelty would be the use of two energy recovery systems: a traditional one, recovering the kinetic energy when braking; and another never seen before with a generator activated by the exhaust gases of the combustion engine. This innovative solution would allow the charging of the lithium-ion batteries while accelerating. The combustion engine would be a small 2-litre V4 with direct fuel injection and turbocharged, putting out 500bhp. This conventional engine would drive the rear axle, while a 400bhp electrical engine would drive the forward axle, powered by the batteries.

Many technical challenges were present in this audacious project, from the global management of all the systems, to the tight control of fuel consumption limited according to the electrical power class chosen. The car went out on track for the first time at the Weissach test circuit in June 2013, in order to undertake performance and endurance tests on varied tracks. This phase of testing concluded in December 2013.

Nick Tandy, Earl Bamber and Nico Hulkenberg celebrate their victory with the Porsche 919 hybrid in the 2015 24 Hours of Le Mans.

The cutaway drawings of the 919 hybrid show its propulsion and energy systems.

The 919 hybrid was formally presented to the public on 14 December 2013, with Porsche pointing out that the car would not only be a competitor in motor sport but also a test bed for innovative technologies, thinking about their future application in series models commercialized by the brand. The 919 made its competition debut in April 2014 at the 6 Hours of Silverstone. In this 'learning year', it achieved several podium finishes and actually won the last race of the WEC[48] Championship in São Paulo.

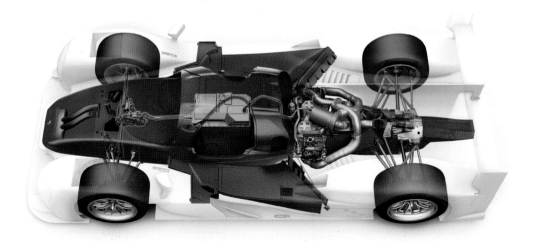

Porsche 919 hybrid still with its 'camouflage' during a test session.

For 2015, the car was profoundly altered, even though it kept a similar look, both at the chassis and bodywork level, as well as its combustion engine and other energy units. Porsche decided to move into the 8 Megajoules class (it was the only brand to do so), which constituted a new challenge for all the electrical and electronic parts, but also for the combustion engine whose consumption would have to be even more limited. Porsche admitted a total power of around the 1,000bhp for the 919. Remarkable!

The year of 2015 was one of great success, not only for the extraordinary win in the 24 Hours of Le Mans but also for the six victories in the eight races of the championship, which allowed the marque and the drivers Mark Webber, Brendon Hartley and Timo Bernhard to become World Endurance Champions. For the fans and enthusiasts of the marque, especially those who had experienced its successes in the twentieth century, these were unforgettable and invigorating moments!

19 MAY 2016, ZUFFENHAUSEN, GERMANY

After sixteen months, I'm back 'home' because my Porschist friend is once again in the Porsche Museum. My mission with him is coming to an end, as his book is almost finished and that's the reason why he is here. He has come to visit the historic archives, with the goal of getting photographs to illustrate his (and my!) stories, as well as to analyse relevant documents to clear up some doubts about a couple of events. I see that he is very happy, not only because his project is almost concluded, but also for the very special meaning to him of being here, inside the 'heart' and 'memory' of the marque.

With his research almost concluded, he decides to visit during his lunch break the temporary exhibition that the museum is showing: 'The Transaxle Era. From the 924 to the 928', which logically both interests him and holds a very special meaning. He goes up the escalator that gives access to the exhibition and looks around, in this familiar space, to decide where to start his visit.

I feel it's time to say goodbye, happy on the one hand because I think that our 'symbiosis' worked, allowing me to tell some of my adventures in my very special world, but also a bit sad as is always the case when we say goodbye to

The Porsche Museum lobby seen from the escalator leading to the exhibition floor. In front we can see on the ground floor the museum workshop and above it the Porsche Archives Department.

The Porsche Museum is the best place to understand and admire the marque's special 'DNA', born eight decades ago and which goes on captivating customers, drivers and enthusiasts all over the world.

a great friend, not knowing if we will meet again. But such is the way it must be, as it is here where I belong, in one car or another of the many present that tell the eighty years of Porsche's history. I don't exactly know which will be my immediate 'habitat', because I'm once again depending on that usual gesture by my 'friend'! Which car will he choose to 'greet' today with his touch? I don't know, but it isn't really important, since what does matter to me is to be able to remain in the middle of this very special 'DNA'. Whether it is in the museum, at a classic car event, at a fan meeting, or at a race, it will always be a huge pleasure!

NOTES

CHAPTER 1

1. 60K10 was the number of the project assigned to the car. The number '60' refers to the chassis type used in the KDF-Volkswagen, the 'K' indicates that it has a special body and the '10' is the number assigned to this specific variant.

CHAPTER 2

2. Probably Ferdinand Porsche, Erwin Komenda (designer-engineer), Josef Mickl (engineer and aerodynamic specialist) and Karl Rabe (chief engineer).
3. Porsche subcontracted the coachbuilder Reutter to build the aluminium 60K10 body.
4. The project 114 was for a sophisticated racing car with a 1500cc supercharged V10 central engine, with a two-seat coupé body. This car was never built, but its design was the basis for the 60K10.
5. Probably the Swiss Rupprecht Von Senger
6. Piero Dusio was the wealthy Italian owner of Cisitalia Automobili and a passionate advocate of motor racing, aiming to build a Formula One car to beat Alfa Romeo and Maserati.
7 Porsche subcontracted the assembly of the first 356 cabriolets assembling to Beutler (a Swiss coachbuilder).

CHAPTER 3

8. The car's best race lap on the 8.38-mile (13.49km) circuit was 5min 44sec, at an average of 87.6mph (140.9km/h), which was remarkable for a car with such a small engine.
9. Professor Porsche had died on 30 January 1951.
10. Charles Faroux was French and an old friend of Professor Porsche. He had a major role on his release from captivity in 1947.
11. Automobile Club de l'Ouest, the organizer of the 24 Hours of Le Mans.
12. The 550 was the first Porsche designed and built specifically for competition. Its aluminium body rested on a simple tubular chassis. It raced for the first time in 1953 at the Nürburgring and appeared at Le Mans in a coupé version, with two cars. The team of Richard von Frankenberg/Paul Frère won its class, followed by the 'sister' car of Hans Herrmann/Walter Glöckler. These 550s used engines (1500 Super) developed from those used in the 356. The famous 547 engine was still in the final stages of development and would begin to be used in 1954. This engine was also known as 'Fuhrmann', the name of its creator, developing at the beginning 110bhp, which represented an increase of almost 30bhp, making the 550 a highly competitive racing machine.
13. 'Attention, attention, one minute!'
14. 'Five, four, three, two, one …'
15. Porsche presented in this race the 550A, which was distinguished by having a much more elaborate chassis and efficient rear suspension than the original version, as well as a more aerodynamic body. The engine had also evolved to the 547/1 version, now developing 135bhp.
16. The 550 arrived in Sicily without any paint on it, showing its 'rough' aluminium body.

CHAPTER 4

17. Porsche and Ferrari had to enrol their cars 'unofficially' due to legal divergences between their fuel sponsors (respectively Shell and BP) and the official fuel supplier (Amoco) of the race.
18. Remarkably, Edgar Barth, during the race, managed to push the car to the pits after losing the right rear wheel on the track. While he still lost a lot of time and positions, this heroic effort allowed him to get to the finish and win the 2000cc class.
19. 'Grandmother'.
20. Porsche had to change from 901 to 911 because Peugeot had already registered the use of three-digit numbers with a zero in the middle.
21. Butzi Porsche created the company Porsche Design Studio in 1972, after the decision by Ferry Porsche that his company would have an independent executive direction without family members. In his new company, later transferred to Zell am See, he dedicated himself to the creation and design of the most diverse items, with the smoking pipes and watches bearing the Porsche Design brand quickly becoming famous. He continued to be a voice that was heard and respected in the company created by his grandfather, in later years being nominated as the Honorary President for the Supervising Council.
22. Fédération Internationale de l'Automobile.
23. The 911 R had already proved itself in endurance races by winning in August the Marathon de la Route, which was run at the Nürburgring circuit for eighty-four hours. It was a very hard race, not only for its length and the track on which it was run, but also for its demanding regulations. Penalty laps were stipulated according to the time spent in pit stops and if there was any malfunction on the circuit only the driver was allowed to make the repair. Thus it was without a doubt the toughest endurance race of the time. Porsche decided to participate and ended up winning the race with a 911 R driven by Hans Herrmann, Jochen Neerpasch and Vic Elford, having driven 6,155 miles (9,905km) during the three and a half days of racing, at an average of 73.2mph (117.8km/h). It is worth emphasizing that the 911 R used an innovative gearbox, the Sportmatic, which Porsche had launched as an option in its 911 series, as the brand wanted to prove its good performance and endurance.
24. The 906, also known as Carrera 6, was the first racing car for which Ferdinand Piech was fully responsible. It debuted in competition at the 24 Hours of Daytona 1966, where it achieved sixth place with Herrmann/Linge. That year, in addition to several victories in its class, it won the Targa Florio with Willy Mairesse/Herbert Müller and obtained fourth, fifth, sixth and seventh places at the 24 Hours of Le Mans, winning its class, behind the powerful Ford GT 40s, but in front of the Ferrari V12. The 906 used the 901/20 engine, which was a development of the engine used in the 911, outputting 220bhp, and its body was completely made of glass-fibre, thus allowing a low total weight of 1,378lb (625kg) which made it very competitive. Fifty-eight units were built, being very successful in the hands of private drivers for several years, in either speed or hill-climb races and even in some rallies.

25. The 910 was an interim model only used by the factory in 1967. It was lighter than the 906 with a more aerodynamic body and it was the first Porsche using 13-inch rims with centre-lock hubs. The 907 could use the six (901/21) or eight (771/0) cylinder engines. It had a short racing life competing for the factory, but nevertheless it gave Porsche victory in 1967 at the Targa Florio with Paul Hawkins/Rolf Stommelen and at the 1,000km Nürburgring with Schütz/Buzzetta. It was also victorious in the European Hill Climb Championship with Gerhard Mitter. The hill-climb races were in fact the main goal for which the 910 was designed, based on the 906 (no.10 chassis), which was deeply modified for that purpose. The 910 chassis and body used in hill-climb races were so optimized that they could reach a super-light weight of 927lb (420kg) with the 8-cylinder engine.

26. Jürgen Barth, son of the great driver Edgar Barth, was an engineer and later also a racing driver, who was beginning his career in the racing department.

CHAPTER 5

27. '50 metres, right 60, Attention! Ice!, 40 metres, 50 left.'

28. The idea of the four aces was meant to remind and pay homage to Ferdinand Porsche, who designed a small sports car for Austro-Daimler, named 'Sascha', in accordance with the name of his mentor (Count Sascha von Korolov). Four cars were enrolled for the Targa Florio race in 1922 and each one had the symbol of each ace from a card deck painted on them. All four cars completed the difficult race, with the best of them winning its race class.

29. 'Gentlemen, [the drivers] place your bets!'

30. 'This is France Inter radio broadcast … we now call on our reporter on the 24 hours of Le Mans … after ten hours of the race …'

31. 'Porsche no.23 now stops at the pits … it leaves now still in first position …'.

32. This record remained unbeatable for thirty-nine years!

33. One must highlight that the Porsche no.59 drove 2,548 miles (4,100km) in the 24 hours, at an average of 106.24mph (170.95km/h), which is remarkable when we compare it with the distance driven by the victorious 917 of Rodriguez/Kinnunen, which in 1970 achieved only 210 miles (338km) more.

34. Porsche had already won in 1976 with the 936 of Ickx/van Lennep and would win again in 1981 with an improved version (936/81) driven by Ickx/Bell.

35. The speeches come from Porsche's *Christophorus* magazine.

CHAPTER 6

36. Unfortunately, the 356/1 suffered an accident when it was lowered from the aeroplane and could not be displayed at the event.

37. This decision was justified by the fact that the LMP1 regulations clearly favoured diesel engines, which logically was not appealing for Porsche.

38. American Le Mans Series.

39. Porsche Motorsport North America.

40. Porsche Club 924-944-968 France.

41. Ferdinand Alexander 'Butzi' Porsche passed away on 5 April 2012.

42. The Porsche tractors were made by the Allgaier Company between 1950 and 1956 and by the Mannesmann company between 1956 and 1963.

43. Factory II.

44. Westfallichen Porsche Club Hohensyburg.

45. Otto Mathé lost part of his right arm in a motorcycle accident in 1934.

46. Porsche developed a new car to compete in the GT1 category from 1996. The bodywork was based on the 911 (model 993) with a twin-turbo 3200cc, 4 valves per cylinder, water-cooled engine putting out 600bhp. The model that won in 1998 had bodywork somewhat different from the original, making the most of the category's regulations.

47. Due to the length of the circuit three safety cars are used; they are strategically placed and come out on to the track simultaneously when necessary.

48. World Endurance Championship.

BIBLIOGRAPHY

BOOKS

Porsche, Ferry and Molter, Gunther, *Cars are my life* (Patrick Stephens, 1989)
Ludvigsen, Karl, *Porsche, Excellence was expected* (Bentley, 2008)
Ludvigsen, Karl, *Porsche, Origin of the Species* (Bentley, 2012)
Boschen, Lothar and Barth, Jurgen, *The Porsche Book* (Patrick Stephens, 1978)
Morgan, Peter, *Porsche in Motorsport* (Haynes, 2000)

Mezger, Hans and Morgan, Peter, *Porsche and Me* (PMM Books, 2012)

PERIODICALS

Christophorus – *Porsche Magazine*, Dr. Ing. h.c. F.Porsche AG
Excellence, the Magazine about Porsche, Ross Periodicals Inc.
L'Automobile magazine, Motor Press France
Flat6 Magazine, Flat 6 Éditions SAS
Autosport, Britain's Motor Sporting Weekly, Autosport Media UK

INDEX

RELATED TITLES FROM CROWOOD

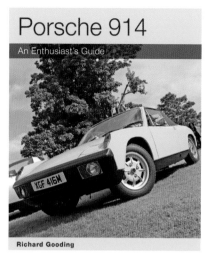

Porsche 914 – An Enthusiast's Guide
RICHARD GOODING
ISBN 978 1 78500 151 2
160pp, 220 illustrations

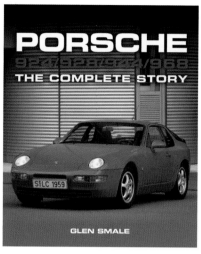

Porsche 924/928/944/968
GLEN SMALE
ISBN 978 1 78500 039 3
192pp, 300 illustrations

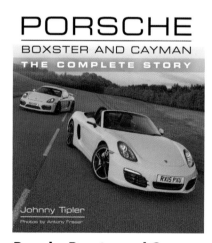

Porsche Boxster and Cayman
JOHNNY TIPLER
ISBN 978 1 78500 211 3
192pp, 400 illustrations

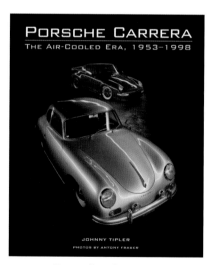

Porsche Carrera
JOHNNY TIPLER
ISBN 978 1 84797 699 4
272pp, 410 illustrations

In case of difficulty ordering, please contact the Sales Office:

The Crowood Press, Ramsbury, Wiltshire SN8 2HR UK

Tel: 44 (0) 1672 520320   enquiries@crowood.com   www.crowood.com